The Family Circle
FAVOURITE
CAKES
COOK BOOK

The Family Circle
FAVOURITE
CAKES
COOK BOOK

HAMLYN

NOTES

1 Level spoon measurements are used in all recipes. When making cakes it is important to use British standard measuring spoons (1 tablespoon = 15 ml; 1 teaspoon = 5 ml). Small sets of measuring spoons are readily available from kitchenware shops and large supermarkets.

2 Both metric and imperial measurements are given. Use only one set of measurements.

3 Eggs are size 3 unless otherwise stated.

4 Milk is full-fat unless otherwise stated.

5 Ovens should always be preheated to the specified temperature. As a general guideline, if using a fan-assisted oven, reduce the stated temperature by 10°C – but always refer to the manufacturer's instructions for adjusting cooking times and temperatures.

6 Before you start cooking, read through the whole recipe. Follow the guidelines given in the introduction on pages 6-11, and don't cut corners when preparing tins or cake mixtures.

7 Some silver and gold cake-decorating paints are inedible – always check the label before buying.

8 Preparation times do not include decorating, because an experienced cake decorator will need considerably less time than a novice.

ACKNOWLEDGEMENTS

Recipes created by **Sally Mansfield, Lauren Floodgate, Matthew Drennan**
Art Director **Jacqui Small**
Executive Art Editor **Penny Stock**
Designers **Paul Tilby, Clare White**
Commissioning Editor **Susan Haynes**
Editors **Sasha Judelson, Maggie Ramsay, Kathy Steer**
Production Controller **Melanie Frantz**
Photographers **Karl Adamson, David Armstrong, Clint Brown, Nick Carman,
Anthony Gould-Davies, James Duncan, Ferguson Hill, Dave Jordan, Alan Newnham,
Ian O'Leary, Tony Robins, Simon Smith, Clive Streeter**
Stylists **Madeleine Brehaut, Suzy Gittins, Philomena Michaels,
Felicity Salter, Wei Tang, Judy Williams**
Indexer **Hilary Bird**

First published in Great Britain in 1995
by Hamlyn
an imprint of Reed Consumer Books Limited
Michelin House, 81 Fulham Road, London SW3 6RB
and Auckland, Melbourne, Singapore and Toronto
Copyright © 1995 Reed International Books

ISBN 0 600 58590 5
A CIP catalogue record for this book is available from the British Library
Produced by Mandarin Offset
Printed and bound in Hong Kong

Contents

Introduction

Over the years the Family Circle cookery team have created many stunning cakes. This delightful book brings you a selection of the best, from celebration and novelty cakes to favourite teatime treats.

Some are simple to make; others are elaborately designed and will appeal to the more experienced cook. However, there is no reason why even a beginner should not be able to produce any of the cakes in this book: they have all been tested by the Family Circle cookery team and are clearly laid out, step by step. Read through the following pages, don't cut corners, and you should have successful results every time.

Here's to happy baking!

Maggi Altham
Associate Editor

Sally Mansfield
Food and Drink Editor

ESSENTIAL EQUIPMENT & ACCESSORIES

Whatever cake you are making you will need certain equipment – most of which you should find in your own kitchen. The keen cake-maker who likes to practise a variety of decorating techniques will find specific accessories will help give better results. As you progress with your cake-making skills, you will find you need a selection of more specialist equipment.

BASICS

- Bowls and tins in various sizes; accurate measuring spoons, jugs and scales; wooden spoons for creaming butter, whisks for beating eggs and cream; a large metal spoon for folding in egg whites and flour.
- A wire rack is essential to prevent cakes from becoming soggy as they cool.
- Palette knives (good quality, flexible, stainless steel) for spreading buttercream and royal icing over cakes. Small, sharp knives for cutting fondant icing.
- Pastry brushes: do not be tempted to buy cheaply, as the bristles may fall out.
- Cake boards, essential for most celebration and novelty cakes, should be about 5 cm (2 inches) larger than the cake tin.
- Piping bags, in linen or plastic, are essential when dealing with large quantities of icing. Piping guns are useful for a variety of piping techniques. Piping nozzles come in many shapes and sizes; the recipe will tell you which type you need.
- Cocktail sticks are useful when modelling novelty cakes, and for several fondant decorating techniques.

SPECIALIST EQUIPMENT

- Plastic cake smoothers are invaluable hand tools for smoothing the surface of fondant-iced cakes.
- A metal cake-decorating ruler is ideal for smoothing royal icing.
- Paintbrushes in various sizes: you may need fine bristles for painting small decorations. Choose good-quality brushes, otherwise the bristles may fall out.
- Rolling pins, much smaller and lighter than the standard type, are used for rolling out small quantities of fondant icing.
- Metal icing crimpers are useful for marking subtle decorations on fondant-iced or marzipan-covered cakes (see Dark Battenburg, page 108).
- Shaped cutters make it easy to cut large numbers of regularly shaped leaves, petals or flowers out of fondant icing.
- Ready-made stamens on fine wire (available from specialist cake-decorating outlets) give a professional touch to floral decorations.

TECHNIQUES AND TIPS

Before you start

- Read each recipe carefully and always use the recommended tin size for a successful result.

- For sponge cakes, and for other cakes when indicated, line the tin with greaseproof paper (see right). For fruit cakes, line the tin with greaseproof paper, then make a brown paper collar for added protection during cooking.

- Check dried fruit for stalks and impurities before adding it to the cake mixture. If necessary, wash the fruit, pat dry with kitchen paper and leave to dry overnight (unless soaking in alcohol).

- If very sticky, glacé cherries should be washed to remove excess syrup, dried on kitchen paper and then dipped in flour.

- When measuring sticky ingredients, such as golden syrup, first dip the measuring spoon in hot water. The ingredient will then slip off the spoon more readily.

- When making a fruit cake, always cook the cake immediately after mixing. If left to stand before cooking the raw mixture will start to ferment slightly.

- Unless otherwise stated, cakes should always be cooked on the middle shelf of the oven.

- It is advisable not to open the oven door to look at a cake while it is cooking until three-quarters of the time given in the recipe has elapsed.

- Once cooked, leave fruit cakes to cool for 5-10 minutes before removing from the tin. Other cakes should be left in the tin for anything from 30 seconds to 10 minutes – see individual recipes.

- Wrap fruit cakes in the greaseproof paper in which they were cooked and plenty of foil. Store in a tin in a cool dark place.

- Fondant-iced cakes can serve a large number of people, as only small helpings are needed. A guide to serving quantities is given in the chart on page 10.

Decorating tips

- Always roll out almond paste and fondant on a surface lightly dusted with icing sugar.

- It is often recommended that marzipanned cakes are left to dry before icing. This is to avoid almond oils seeping through and spoiling the icing, but this occurs only after long storage.

- To fill a piping bag with royal icing, use a round-bladed knife, and half-fill the bag with icing (do not overfill), pressing the icing down into the bag.

- Drying times for fondant icing are given at various stages of the decorating process. This allows the icing to firm up, but is not always necessary: many of the cakes in this book can be decorated on the day they are to be eaten. However, showpiece cakes such as wedding cakes may need up to a week to dry.

- For a finishing touch, tie a piece of narrow ribbon around the cake board, holding it in place with a few dabs of royal icing.

- Once decorated, never store an iced cake in the refrigerator, as the fondant will become moist and the colours will run. Store in large boxes in a dark cool place.

- Gum tragacanth is used to make fondant figures and flowers set rock-hard so they do not 'wilt'. Be prepared to work quickly, as it does not take long to set. Usually sold in powdered form: to every 450 g (1 lb) fondant add ½ teaspoon gum tragacanth.

- Use a cocktail stick to add colour gradually to icing, until you are sure of the effect; knead until the icing is evenly coloured.

- Paste food colour is most versatile: a very little gives an intense colour and it can be applied direct to icing with a paintbrush. Gel colours (from specialist cake-decorating outlets) are even more intense. Liquid food colouring can be used only for pale colours, and may run if applied direct.

GREASING AND LINING A CAKE TIN

Brush the sides and base of the tin lightly but thoroughly with sunflower or other neutral-flavoured oil. Line the base with a piece of greaseproof paper cut to the correct size.

Measure the circumference of the tin with string. Cut a strip of paper, about 5 cm (2 inches) deeper than the tin, to the required length. Fold over a 2.5 cm (1 inch) rim and make diagonal snips along the rim.

Place the paper strip around the inside of the tin, making sure the snipped edges are flush to the corner. Cover the base of the tin with a second piece of greaseproof paper.

MAKING A PIPING BAG AND FITTING A NOZZLE

Cut a large piece of greaseproof paper, measuring about 25 cm (10 inches) square. Fold over and cut out a triangle. Mark the corners A, B, C. Fold corner A up to corner B.

Twist corner A over B to form a cone, then bring corner C around the front of the cone to the back of B. Fold over and secure the cone shape with a piece of sticky tape.

To fit a nozzle, cut the paper piping bag at an angle, about 5 mm (¼ inch) from the point; drop in the nozzle. Fill with icing, then fold over the top of the bag, bring the corners in to the centre, and fold over again.

COVERING A CAKE WITH ALMOND PASTE

Throughout the book we refer to almond paste. This is marzipan, available in white or yellow. Before using, knead the almond paste on a surface lightly dusted with icing sugar, until it is soft and pliable.

Place the cake upside down on the cake board, so that the top is level. After filling the gaps around the base of the cake with a rope of almond paste (see right), brush the cake all over with warmed, sieved apricot jam.

ROUND CAKES
Roll out the almond paste to a circle 10 cm (4 inches) larger than the cake. Roll the trimmings into a long rope, and push this around the base of the cake to fill in any gaps, then smooth with a palette knife. Brush the cake with jam. Run your forearms under the almond paste and lift it over the cake. Smooth the almond paste with the palm of your hand and finish with a cake smoother.

SQUARE CAKES
Cut out a square of almond paste 2.5 cm (1 inch) larger than the cake. Roll the trimmings into a long rope and use to even out any gaps around the base of the cake. Put the square of almond paste on top and trim. Measure the circumference of the cake with string. Roll out a piece of almond paste to the required length. Trim the strip of almond paste to the depth of the cake, roll it up gently, then unroll it around the cake.

Basic Cake Mixtures

Rich Fruit Cake Mixture

Square tin size	12 cm (5 inch)	15 cm (6 inch)	18 cm (7 inch)	20 cm (8 inch)	23 cm (9 inch)	25 cm (10 inch)	28 cm (11 inch)
Round tin size	15 cm (6 inch)	18 cm (7 inch)	20 cm (8 inch)	23 cm (9 inch)	25 cm (10 inch)	28 cm (11 inch)	30 cm (12 inch)
Serves	12-16	16-20	20-28	32-36	40-48	68-81	80-92
Currants	150 g (6 oz)	200 g (7 oz)	275 g (10 oz)	325 g (12 oz)	550 g (1¼ lb)	725 g (1 lb 10 oz)	1.1 kg (2½ lb)
Sultanas	100 g (4 oz)	115 g (4 ½ oz)	165 g (6½ oz)	225 g (8 oz)	275 g (10 oz)	475 g (1 lb 1 oz)	550 g (1¼ lb)
Raisins (seedless)	75 g (3 oz)	90 g (3½ oz)	115 g (4½ oz)	150 g (6 oz)	225 g (8 oz)	375 g (13 oz)	400 g (14 oz)
Glacé cherries	50 g (2 oz)	50 g (2 oz)	75 g (3 oz)	115 g (4½ oz)	150 g (6 oz)	250 g (9 oz)	275 g (10 oz)
Mixed peel (chopped)	25 g (1 oz)	25 g (1 oz)	50 g (2 oz)	75 g (3 oz)	90 g (3½ oz)	125 g (5 oz)	200 g (7 oz)
Ground almonds	25 g (1 oz)	25 g (1 oz)	50 g (2 oz)	75 g (3 oz)	90 g (3½ oz)	125 g (5 oz)	200 g (7 oz)
Lemon rind (grated)	a little	a little	a little	¼ lemon	¼ lemon	½ lemon	½ lemon
Plain flour	125 g (5 oz)	150 g (6 oz)	200 g (7 oz)	300 g (11 oz)	400 g (14 oz)	575g (1lb 5 oz)	675 g (1½ lb)
Ground mixed spice	¼ teaspoon	¼ teaspoon	½ teaspoon	½ teaspoon	1 teaspoon	1 teaspoon	2 teaspoons
Ground cinnamon	¼ teaspoon	¼ teaspoon	½ teaspoon	½ teaspoon	1 teaspoon	1 teaspoon	2 teaspoons
Butter	115g (4½ oz)	125 g (5 oz)	150 g (6 oz)	250 g (9 oz)	325 g (12 oz)	500 g (1 lb 2 oz)	575 g (1 lb 5 oz)
Brown sugar	115 g (4½ oz)	125 g (5 oz)	150 g (6 oz)	250 g (9 oz)	325 g (12 oz)	500 g (1 lb 2 oz)	675 g (1 lb 5 oz)
Eggs (size 3)	2	2½	3	4	6	9	11
Brandy	1 tablespoon	1 tablespoon	1-2 tablespoons	2 tablespoons	2-3 tablespoons	3 tablespoons	3 tablespoons
Time (approximately)	2½-3 hours	2½-3½ hours	3-3½ hours	3½-4½ hours	4-4½ hours	5½-6 hours	7½ hours
Weight when cooked	1 kg (2¼ lb)	1.25 kg (2¾ lb)	1.75 kg (3½ lb)	2.25 kg (4½ lb)	3 kg (6 lb)	4.5 kg (9 lb)	5.75 kg (11½ lb)

Sponge Cake Mixture

Square tin size	12 cm (5 inch)	15 cm (6 inch)	18 cm (7 inch)	20 cm (8 inch)	23 cm (9 inch)
Round tin size	15 cm (6 inch)	18 cm (7 inch)	20 cm (8 inch)	23 cm (9 inch)	25 cm (10 inch)
Butter	100 g (4 oz)	125 g (5 oz)	150 g (6 oz)	275 g (10 oz)	400 g (14 oz)
Caster sugar	100 g (4 oz)	125 g (5 oz)	150 g (6 oz)	275 g (10 oz)	400 g (14 oz)
Eggs (size 3)	2	2½	3	5	7
Self-raising flour	100 g (4 oz)	125 g (5 oz)	150 g (6 oz)	325 g (12 oz)	450 g (1 lb)
Time	50 minutes	50 minutes	50 minutes	1 hour	1¼ hours

HOW TO MAKE A FRUIT CAKE

1 Grease the cake tin and line with greaseproof paper (see page 9). Tie a double thickness of brown paper around the outside of the tin.

2 Put the currants, sultanas and raisins into a bowl. Cut the cherries in half, add to the bowl, then stir in the peel, almonds and lemon rind.

3 Sift the flour and spices together.

4 In a separate bowl, beat the butter and sugar together until light and fluffy. Beat the eggs together, then add to the butter mixture a little at a time, beating well after each addition.

5 Fold in the flour and spice mixture with a metal spoon. Stir in the fruit mixture and brandy.

6 Spoon the mixture into the prepared tin. Cover the top of the cake with foil to prevent overbrowning. Place in a preheated oven, 150°C (300°F), Gas Mark 2, for the time stated in the chart (left).

7 Check that the cake is cooked by inserting a skewer into the centre. If the skewer comes out clean the cake is ready.

HOW TO MAKE A SPONGE CAKE

1 Grease the cake tin and line with greaseproof paper (see page 9).

2 Beat the butter and caster sugar together until light and fluffy.

3 Beat in the eggs, a little at a time, beating in a little flour after each addition of egg.

4 Fold in the remaining flour, then spoon the mixture into the prepared cake tin.

5 Place in a preheated oven, 160°C (325°F), Gas Mark 3, for the time stated in the chart (left), until the sponge is well risen and golden.

CAKES FOR UNUSUALLY SHAPED TINS

When using unusually shaped tins, fill them with water to the required cooked cake level and measure the amount of water used in a jug. For every 600 ml (1 pint) of liquid you will need a cake mixture made up of the following ingredients:

FRUIT CAKE

125 g (5 oz) currants

50 g (2 oz) sultanas

50 g (2 oz) seedless raisins

12 glacé cherries

25 g (1 oz) chopped mixed peel

25 g (1 oz) ground almonds

a little grated lemon rind

100 g (4 oz) plain flour

¼ teaspoon ground mixed spice

¼ teaspoon ground cinnamon

75 g (3 oz) butter or margarine

75 g (3 oz) soft brown sugar

1½ eggs (size 3)

1 tablespoon (15 ml) brandy

SPONGE CAKE

50 g (2 oz) butter

50 g (2 oz) caster sugar

1 egg (size 3)

50 g (2 oz) self-raising flour

Celebration Cakes

SIMNEL CAKE

1 Grease and line the base and sides of a 20 cm (8 inch) round, deep, loose-bottomed cake tin with a double piece of greaseproof paper.

2 Sift the flour, baking powder and spices into a large bowl.

3 Beat the butter and brown sugar together until light and fluffy. Add the eggs, one at a time, beating well after each addition. Using a metal spoon, fold in the flour mixture.

4 Fold in the port, milk, fruit, cherries and lemon rind. Spoon half of the mixture into the tin.

5 Roll out 225 g (8 oz) of the white almond paste to a 20 cm (8 inch) circle. Ease it over the cake mixture, then cover with the remaining mixture and level the surface.

6 Wrap a double thickness of brown paper around the outside of the tin and tie with string so it comes 2.5 cm (1 inch) above the rim. Place in a preheated oven, 150°C (300°F), Gas Mark 2, for 2 hours. Cover with foil and cook for a further 30 minutes, or until a

skewer inserted into the centre comes out clean. Cool in the tin.

7 When cold, turn out the cake. Brush the top with warmed, sieved apricot jam. Roll out the remaining white almond paste to a thickness of 5 mm (¼ inch). Repeat with the yellow almond paste. Cut 10 strips, each 23 x 1.5 cm (9 x ¾ inch), from each of the colours.

8 Lay the white strips side by side on a surface lightly dusted with icing sugar. Weave in the yellow strips to create a basket effect. Lift the almond paste lattice over the cake, using 2 fish slices. Trim around the edge. Knead the yellow almond paste trimmings and divide into 11. Roll into balls and gently push into place around the edge of the cake. Tie a length of yellow ribbon around the cake.

Serves 12

PREPARATION TIME: **20** MINUTES

COOKING TIME: 2½ HOURS

OVEN TEMPERATURE: **150°C (300°F),**

GAS MARK **2**

275 g (10 oz) plain flour

2 teaspoons baking powder

1 teaspoon ground allspice

½ teaspoon ground cinnamon

215 g (7½ oz) butter, softened

215 g (7½ oz) soft dark brown sugar

6 eggs

3 tablespoons (45 ml) port

3 tablespoons (45 ml) milk

500 g (1 lb 2 oz) mixed dried fruit

75 g (3 oz) glacé cherries, halved

grated rind of 1 lemon

550 g (1¼ lb) white almond paste

1 tablespoon apricot jam, warmed
and sieved

325 g (12 oz) yellow almond paste

icing sugar, to dust

YOU WILL ALSO NEED

70 cm (28 inches) yellow satin ribbon

BABY'S FIRST BIRTHDAY

1 egg white

1 teaspoon (5 ml) lemon juice

225 g (8 oz) icing sugar, sifted

25 cm (10 inch) round fruit cake,
  covered with almond paste

1.4 kg (3 lb) ready-to-roll
  fondant icing

lemon and fuchsia pink or blue
  food colouring

YOU WILL ALSO NEED

25 cm (10 inch) round silver
  cake board

small flower cutter

1 duck- and 1 teddy-shaped button

20 cm x 5 mm (8 inches x ¼ inch) white
  satin ribbon

66 cm x 4 cm (26 inches x 1½ inch) and
  86.5 cm x 2.5 cm (34 inches x
    1 inch) pale pink or blue satin ribbon

piping gun or bag set

1 First make the royal icing: put the egg white, lemon juice and icing sugar in a bowl and beat together until smooth. Cover with damp greaseproof paper and put the bowl in a large polythene bag in the refrigerator until required.

2 Put the cake on the board. Colour 1.1 kg (2½ lb) of the fondant pale lemon. Roll out and cover the cake. Trim the base. Colour 125 g (5 oz) of the fondant pale pink or blue. Roll out 25 g (1 oz) and use to cut out small flowers. Dampen with water and fix around the top edge of the cake.

3 Push the duck button into the icing just below the flowers. Repeat with the teddy bear button around the base of the cake.

4 Shape 2 bootees from 25 g (1 oz) of the pink or blue fondant. Roll out a little of the remaining white (uncoloured) fondant and cut out 2 small rectangles. Dampen the edges and then fix on to each bootee to make a cuff. Carefully pinch together at the front.

5 Cut the 5 mm (¼ inch) ribbon in half and use to tie 2 small bows. Dampen the front of each bootee with a little water and attach a white ribbon bow. Use the 4 cm (1½ inch) wide pink or blue ribbon to tie a large bow and set aside.

6 Use 75 g (3 oz) of pink or blue fondant to shape the teddy's legs, arms, body, head and ears, as shown below. Use white fondant to make the features and paws and attach with a little water. Fix the head, arms and legs on the body with water. Leave to dry, then position on the cake with the bootees.

7 Roll out the pink or blue fondant trimmings and cut out the baby's name. Fix to the cake with a little water. Using a fine plain nozzle, outline the edges of the letters with royal icing. Tie the 2.5 cm (1 inch) wide pink or blue ribbon around the cake and attach the bow with a little royal icing.

Press shaped buttons into the icing to make a design around the cake.

Shape the bootees from pink or blue fondant; trim with white fondant and tiny ribbon bows.

Shape the teddy from pink and blue fondant; use white fondant for the features and paws.

TEENAGE BIRTHDAY

20 cm (8 inch) round fruit cake or
   sponge cake, covered with
   almond paste
1.2 kg (2 lb 10 oz) ready-to-roll
   fondant icing
orange, blue, yellow, green, red and
   violet food colouring
¼ teaspoon gum tragacanth

YOU WILL ALSO NEED
25 cm (10 inch) round silver
   cake board
4.5 cm (1¾ inch) star cutter
3 cm (1¼ inch) star cutter
26 x 20 cm (8 inch) lengths of thin wire
   or thin-gauge florists' wire, covered
   with white florists' tape

1 Roll out 900 g (2 lb) of the fondant to a 40 cm (16 inch) circle. Lift the fondant over the cake and smooth into place. Trim the edges, reserving the trimmings.

2 Knead a little orange food colouring into the remaining 275 g (10 oz) fondant with the gum tragacanth. Roll out the fondant to a circle just larger than the cake. Place on top of the cake and make folds to give a ruffled effect. Pinch the edges to give a delicate finish.

3 Roll out the reserved fondant trimmings and stamp out 8 large and 5 smaller stars. Twist 2 lengths of wire together. Attach some wire to each star, using a little fondant and a little water, as shown, right. Leave to dry overnight.

4 Mix a little water with each of the remaining food colours. Holding the stars by the wire, paint them in different colours. Leave to dry for at least 3 hours.

5 Gently push the ends of the wires through the 'crumpled' fondant, arranging the stars at different heights and angles to give a starburst effect.

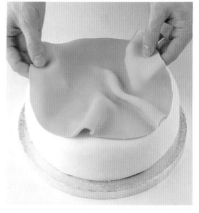

Cut out a circle of coloured fondant, a little larger than the cake. Lift the edges at irregular intervals to give a crumpled effect.

Cut out fondant stars and attach to twisted lengths of florists' wire, using water and a circle of fondant to secure the stars.

When the stars are completely dry, paint them all over in a variety of colours, holding them by the wire. Leave them to dry.

21ST BIRTHDAY

25 cm (10 inch) square fruit cake

2.1 kg (4 lb 10 oz) almond paste

2.1 kg (4 lb 10 oz) ready-to-roll
    fondant icing

pink, yellow, orange, violet and black
    food colouring

YOU WILL ALSO NEED

140 cm x 4.5 cm (56 inches x 1¾ inch)
    each of gold, pink, purple and
    tartan ribbons,

small flower and star cutters

metal sieve

blue tissue paper, shredded

1 small piece white paper

2 cocktail sticks

30 cm (12 inch) square silver
    cake board

1 Cut the fruit cake into 4 squares and divide the almond paste into quarters. Roll out each quarter of almond paste and use to cover the cake quarters. Leave the cakes to dry for 2 days.

2 Divide 1.8 kg (4 lb) of the fondant into quarters. Colour 1 quarter of the fondant pink, 1 yellow, 1 orange and 1 violet. Roll out and cover the 4 cakes. Fold in the excess icing at opposite ends of each cake, like a parcel. Trim the bases neatly. Reserve the pink trimmings and knead into 165 g (6½ oz) of the white fondant. If necessary, add a little more pink colouring to make a flesh colour; reserve.

3 Using a sharp knife, make 2 slits diagonally across the top of the pink cake and fold back the icing to reveal the almond paste. Leave to dry overnight.

4 Cut the gold ribbon into 4, trim one end of each length into a 'V' shape and fix the other end to the base of the pink cake with a little water. Fix the shaped end of the ribbon to the underside of the open flaps. Roll out 75 g (3 oz) of the white fondant and cut out a label,

some stars and flowers. Reserve the label, and fix the stars to the yellow cake and the flowers to the orange cake. Colour the remaining 15 g (½ oz) of fondant black.

5 Use the reserved flesh pink fondant to roll a ball for the head and a tiny nose, and shape the body, arms and hands. Fix together with water. Press the black fondant through a sieve to make the hair. Fix to the head. Paint on the face. Fill the open present with tissue paper and then put the model on top. Cut 2 paper flags. Using black colouring, write on the messages and stick to the cocktail sticks. Press into the model's hands. Wrap the remaining parcel cakes in ribbon. Paint 'Happy 21st' on the label and fix to the violet cake. Arrange the cakes on the cake board.

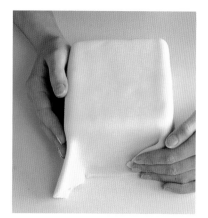

Cover the cakes with fondant icing, folding the ends neatly, like a parcel.

Cut slits in the fondant across the top of the pink cake and open out.

Make the model male or female, with different skin or hair colours, if you like.

ADULT BIRTHDAY

2 egg whites

2 teaspoons (10 ml) lemon juice

450 g (1 lb) icing sugar, sifted

25 cm (10 inch) round fruit cake,
covered with almond paste

1.2 kg (2 lb 10 oz) ready-to-roll
fondant icing

cornflower blue food colouring

YOU WILL ALSO NEED

30 cm (12 inch) round silver
cake board

waxed paper

piping gun or bag set

1 First make the royal icing: put the egg whites and lemon juice in a large bowl and stir together with a fork. Gradually beat in the icing sugar and beat for 10 minutes, until the icing sugar is white and forms soft peaks. Cover with damp grease-proof paper and put the bowl in a polythene bag in the refrigerator.

2 Put the cake on the cake board. Colour 1.1 kg (2½ lb) of the fondant cornflower blue. Roll out the fondant and use it to cover the cake. Trim the base.

3 Using a sharp pencil, trace the outline of 8 bunches of grapes, a cherub, a dancing girl, a tree and 2 potted plants on to a sheet of waxed

paper. Using a fine plain nozzle and royal icing, outline the figures and objects traced on the waxed paper. Leave to dry for 10 minutes. Thin the remaining royal icing with a couple of drops of water. Pipe the thinned royal icing inside the outlines to fill the shapes completely. Leave to dry overnight.

4 Remove the paper from the shapes. Using a little royal icing, fix 8 bunches of grapes around the side of the cake, equally spaced apart. Arrange all the figures and objects on the top of the cake, then fix in place with royal icing.

5 Roll out the remaining fondant thinly and cut 8 strips, each 10 x 1 cm (4 x ½ inch). Twist the strips and fix to the side of the cake with royal icing, draping the strips between the bunches of grapes. Roll the fondant trimmings into 8 small balls, flatten and use to cover the ends of the icing ropes.

Pipe the outlines of your designs in royal icing, then fill with thinned icing.

GOOD LUCK

*25 cm (10 inch) round fruit cake,
    covered with almond paste*
*1.7 kg (3 lb 12 oz) ready-to-roll
    fondant icing*
*Cornish cream, purple, yellow,
    blue, green, pink and black
    food colouring*

<small>YOU WILL ALSO NEED</small>
*30 cm (12 inch) round silver
    cake board*
small leaf cutter
curved icing crimpers

1 Put the cake on the cake board. Colour 1.1 kg (2½ lb) of the fondant Cornish cream. Roll out and cover the cake. Trim the base. Colour 225 g (8 oz) of the fondant purple. Roll out thinly and cut out a large horseshoe. Make nail holes in the horseshoe, then leave to dry.

2 Divide 225 g (8 oz) of the fondant into 8. Leave 1 piece white. Colour the remaining pieces pale yellow, yellow, pale blue, blue, pale green, green and pink. Cut out the leaves and shape the petals. Reserve the green and pink trimmings. Using a little water, fix the flowers and leaves to the horseshoe and cake sides. Fix the horseshoe on the cake with a little water.

3 Colour the remaining fondant black. Shape the cat's head, body, legs and tail as shown, right. Use a little of the reserved green fondant

for the eyes and pink for the nose. Assemble, using a little water. Fix on top of the cake in the middle of the horseshoe.

4 Using icing crimpers as shown below, mark a decorative pattern in the icing around the top edge and base of the cake.

Assemble the cat and leave to dry for at least 1 hour before placing on the cake.

Icing crimpers are an easy way to give a finishing touch to an iced cake.

21

RETIREMENT

1 egg white

1 teaspoon (5 ml) lemon juice

225 g (8 oz) icing sugar, sifted

25 cm (10 inch) square fruit cake,
*   covered with almond paste*

1.8 kg (4 lb) ready-to-roll fondant icing

chestnut, brown, red and golden yellow
*   food colouring*

gold food paint

YOU WILL ALSO NEED

30 cm (12 inch) square silver
*   cake board*

106 cm x 6 cm (42 inches x 2½ inch)
*   gold paper ribbon*

selection of leaf cutters

piping gun or bag set

1 First make the royal icing: put the egg white, lemon juice and icing sugar in a bowl and beat together until smooth. Cover with damp greaseproof paper and put the bowl in a large polythene bag in the refrigerator until required.

2 Put the cake on the cake board. Roll out 1.4 kg (3 lb) of the fondant and cover the cake. Trim the base.

3 Colour 100 g (4 oz) of the fondant pale chestnut. Roll out to a thickness of 5 mm (¼ inch). Cut 2 pieces, each 10 x 7 cm (4 x 3 inches), for the spine and book covers (front and back). Cut a 50 g (2 oz) block of white fondant 1.5 cm (¾ inch) deep and slightly smaller than the book covers. Using a little water, fix this

piece to the back cover and spine. Score lines for the pages on the side of the white block. Put the book on the cake. Cut a 15 cm (6 inch) piece of gold ribbon for the bookmark. Lay the ribbon on the book. Roll out the remaining white fondant and cut a piece the same size as the book block, turn up the top right corner and place on top of the book mark for the front page. Position the front cover of the book and neaten the joins.

4 Divide the remaining fondant into 4 equal pieces. Colour 1 piece dark chestnut, 1 brown, 1 red and 1 golden yellow. Roll each piece out thinly and, using various leaf cutters, cut out several leaves in each colour. Score the veins on the leaves with a sharp knife. Fix the leaves around the top and sides of the cake by dampening them with a little water.

5 Using a fine plain nozzle, pipe the royal icing into ears of corn shapes in between the leaves. Leave to dry.

6 Using gold food paint, paint the ears of corn and the message on the book. Leave to dry. Fix the gold paper ribbon around the cake, using a little royal icing.

Assemble the book, fixing together with water. Mark the 'pages' of the book by scoring the edge of the white fondant with a knife.

Cut out leaves in various shapes and colours, and plan the design by arranging them together before fixing to the cake.

Carefully paint the piped ears of corn in gold – some brands of gold food paint are inedible and best used for decoration only, so check before buying.

WEDDING CAKE

1 egg white

1 teaspoon (5 ml) lemon juice

225 g (8 oz) icing sugar, sifted

25 cm (10 inch) square fruit cake,
   covered with almond paste

1.4 kg (3 lb) ready-to-roll fondant icing

Cornish cream food colouring

4 edible gold balls

YOU WILL ALSO NEED

30 cm (12 inch) square silver
   cake board

265 cm x 5 mm (104 inches x ¼ inch),
   160 cm x 4 cm (62 inches x 1½ inch)
   and 142 cm x 1 cm (56 inches x
   ½ inch) champagne-coloured
   satin ribbons

piping gun or bag set

1 small bunch of fresh rosebuds

1 First make the royal icing: put the egg white, lemon juice and icing sugar in a bowl and beat together until smooth. Cover with damp greaseproof paper and put the bowl in a large polythene bag in the refrigerator until required.

2 Put the cake on the cake board. Colour the fondant Cornish cream. Roll out thinly and cut a 25 cm (10 inch) square. Place on top of the cake and smooth over. Cut the remaining fondant into 4 panels, each 30 x 10 cm (12 x 4 inches). Press the fondant pieces on to the sides of the cake so the pieces overhang 2.5 cm (1 inch) at each end.

Press the overhangs together, then roll outwards.

3 Using a small pointed knife, cut 5 mm (¼ inch) slits in the fondant at regular intervals to make a geometric design on the top and sides of the cake. Cut the 5 mm (¼ inch) ribbon into 1.5 cm (¾ inch) lengths. Using a small sharp knife or a pair of tweezers, insert 1 ribbon length into every pair of slits, leaving a space between each pair.

4 Colour the royal icing Cornish cream. Using a fine plain nozzle, pipe a delicate floral design on the top and sides of the cake.

5 Twist the 4 cm (1½ inch) wide ribbon until it forms a tight tube. Measure around the top of the cake and trim the ribbon to fit. With the raw ends at one corner, fix the ribbon around the edge of the cake using dabs of royal icing. Cut the 1 cm (½ inch) ribbon into 4 equal lengths and tie into small bows. Cut the ends into 'V' shapes and fix the bows and the gold balls to the corners of the cake, using royal icing. Tie the rosebuds into a posy with a length of 4 cm (1½ inch) ribbon. Lay the posy on top of the cake.

To create the 'woven' effect, first make regular slits in the icing, then use a knife or tweezers to push short lengths of ribbon into the slits.

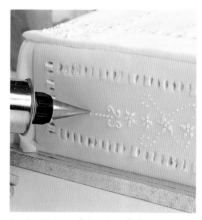

Practise piping your design – it can be kept quite simple – on a piece of greaseproof paper before piping directly on to the cake.

Cover the join between the top and sides of the cake with a piece of satin ribbon, rolled to form a tube. Attach to the cake with royal icing.

Tiered Wedding Cake

FOR A 15 CM (6 INCH) ROUND CAKE

3 tablespoons apricot jam

450 g (1 lb) almond paste

450 g (1 lb) ready-to-roll fondant icing,
coloured champagne

FOR A 23 CM (9 INCH) ROUND CAKE

4 tablespoons apricot jam

900 g (2 lb) almond paste

900 g (2 lb) ready-to-roll fondant icing,
coloured champagne

FOR A 30 CM (12 INCH) ROUND CAKE

6 tablespoons apricot jam

1.8 kg (4 lb) almond paste

1.8 kg (4 lb) ready-to-roll fondant
icing, coloured champagne

TO MAKE THE FLOWERS YOU WILL NEED

1.8 kg (4 lb) ready-to-roll fondant icing

1 teaspoon gum tragacanth

old gold, yellow and leaf green
food colouring

3 cm (1¼ inch) daisy cutter

cocktail sticks

3 cm (1¼ inch) round cutter

rose leaf cutter

YOU WILL ALSO NEED

450 g (1 lb) icing sugar

2 egg whites

piping bag

plain no. 1 and no. 2 nozzles

6 dowelling rods

6 plaster cake pillars

1 Cover the cakes with almond paste, as described on page 9, and then cover with fondant.

2 To make the flowers: knead the fondant until smooth, then add the gum tragacanth and knead thoroughly. Once you have added the gum tragacanth the fondant will harden quickly: read through the instructions to decide whether to make the flowers in batches. Colour 675 g (1½ lb) of the fondant gold. Wrap both the white and gold fondants in clingfilm.

3 To make the daisies: roll out 125 g (5 oz) of the white fondant and stamp out 40 daisies. Roll a cocktail stick over each petal to give a delicate finish. Colour 25 g (1 oz) of the fondant yellow and make the daisy centres. Fill a polythene bag with sugar, make indentations with your finger and sit a daisy in each dent. Leave to dry overnight.

4 Use 225 g (8 oz) of the gold fondant to make 12 roses. For each rose, divide a little fondant into 10 and roll each into a ball the size of a large pea. Using a teaspoon dusted in icing sugar, flatten each ball to form a petal. Roll up like a Swiss roll. Flatten a second ball of fondant and wrap around the first petal, securing it with a little water. Continue with all 10 balls to complete a rose. Break off any excess fondant at the base of the rose. Sit the rose in an egg carton to keep its shape, and leave to dry overnight. Use 225 g (8 oz) of fondant to make

Cut out the daisies using a shaped cutter, then roll the petals with a cocktail stick. Leave to dry on a bag of sugar to give the daisies a slightly curved shape.

To make fondant roses, flatten balls of fondant with the back of a teaspoon, roll up the first petal, then wrap 9 more petals around it.

The large flowers are made up of 5 petals, each rolled with a cocktail stick to give a delicate ruffled effect, and filled with a mass of 'stamens'.

Tiered Wedding Cake

To make arum lilies, cut out white petals and roll out long yellow stamens. Wrap the petals around the stamens and leave to dry on a rolling pin.

Make ivy leaves from triangles of fondant. Cut a nick in the centre and push the corners up, then mark the veins with a knife.

Arrange the flowers and leaves on the 3 cakes and attach with a dab of icing. The cake is assembled in tiers at the wedding.

12 white roses. Use the trimmings to make 6 rosebuds, with only 4 petals instead of 10.

5 To make the large flowers: roll out the remaining gold fondant and stamp out 5 rounds using a 3 cm (1¼ inch) round plain cutter. To form petals, roll a cocktail stick around each round to give a ruffled edge. Stick 5 petals together with a little water. For the stamens, roll the trimmings into small balls (approximately 20 for each flower). Secure with a little water. Make 16 flowers in total. Place each flower in an egg carton to help form the shape, and leave to dry overnight.

6 To make the arum lilies: roll out 325 g (12 oz) of the white fondant and, using a sharp knife, cut out different sized petals. Colour 225 g (8 oz) of the fondant yellow and make the stamens. Lay each stamen in the centre of a petal and wrap the petal around. Secure with a little water. Make 25 lilies in total. Drape over a rolling pin to form the shape, and leave to dry overnight.

7 Colour 75 g (3 oz) of the fondant leaf green and 75 g (3 oz) a darker green. Roll out the lighter green fondant and cut into 2.5 cm (1 inch) strips. Cut the strips into triangles. Cut a nick in each triangle and pinch up the corners to give an ivy leaf shape. Mark the veins with a knife. Make 60 ivy leaves in total.

Roll out the darker green fondant and stamp out 30 rose leaves. Mark the veins with a knife.

8 Cut a strip of greaseproof paper the same height as the side of the large tier and 100 cm (40 inches) long. Hold the paper around the cake and trim to the exact circumference. Mark into 8 equal sections. Draw a semicircle between each mark. Attach the strip to the cake, securing it with pins. Make pinpricks in the icing through the paper, following the semicircles. Repeat with the other 2 tiers. Mix half the icing sugar with 1 egg white and a little water and beat to form a stiff, smooth icing. Using half the icing and a plain no. 2 nozzle, pipe dots around the base of the cakes. Using the remaining icing and a no.1 nozzle, pipe dots along the pinpricks on all 3 tiers. Leave the cakes to dry overnight.

9 Beat together the remaining icing sugar and egg white to form a smooth icing. Arrange the flowers and leaves on the cakes, then fix in place with a little icing.

10 To assemble: push 3 dowelling rods into the large tier and 3 into the middle tier where you want the pillars to stand. Mark the level of the cake on the rods, remove and cut to length. Push the rods back into the cakes. Assemble the cake, standing pillars over the dowelling.

CHRISTENING

1 egg white

1 teaspoon (5 ml) lemon juice

225 g (8 oz) icing sugar, sifted

*30 cm (12 inch) round fruit cake,
    covered with white almond paste*

2 kg (4½ lb) ready-to-roll fondant icing

blue, orange and pink food colouring

1 teaspoon gum tragacanth

1 tablespoon white vegetable fat

YOU WILL ALSO NEED

35 cm (14 inch) round cake board

nonstick baking paper

dressmakers' pin

piping gun

*small and medium plain writing nozzles
    and rope nozzle*

*125 cm x 1 cm (50 inches x ½ inch)
    blue satin ribbon*

1 First make the royal icing: put the egg white, lemon juice and icing sugar in a bowl and beat together until smooth. Cover with damp greaseproof paper and put the bowl in a large polythene bag in the refrigerator until needed.

2 Put the cake on the cake board. Colour 1.8 kg (4 lb) of the fondant pale blue. Roll out the fondant and cover the cake. Trim the base.

3 Knead the gum tragacanth into the remaining blue fondant and roll out on a surface lightly dusted with icing sugar. Stamp out 6 ovals, each about 7 cm (3 inch) deep, and 1 circle, 20 cm (8 inch) in diameter.

Transfer the ovals to a baking sheet covered with nonstick baking paper and set aside.

4 Draw the outline of a stork on to a 7 cm (3 inch) oval of greaseproof paper. Lay the paper on top of 1 of the fondant ovals and mark a stork design in the fondant by pricking around the stork outline with a pin. Repeat on the remaining ovals. Repeat for the fondant circle, using a larger paper stork template.

5 Colour about one-third of the royal icing orange; colour a small amount deep blue and an even smaller amount pale pink. Leave the rest white. Reserve a little of the white icing, keeping it covered, until the next day. Pipe stork designs on to the fondant ovals, using coloured royal icing, as shown below, and a small writing nozzle. Pipe the stork design on to

Pipe the stork designs on to the fondant plaques and leave to dry overnight.

the fondant circle, using a medium writing nozzle, but this time add a baby in a nappy. Leave to dry overnight.

6 Knead the white vegetable fat into the remaining white fondant, until the texture feels smooth. Using a piping gun fitted with a rope nozzle, carefully pipe 1 x 63 cm (25 inch) length; 1 x 105 cm (42 inch) length and 6 x 18 cm (7 inch) length ropes. Alternatively, roll out the fondant into long thin ropes and twist together in pairs. Attach the ropes around the base of the cake and around each stork plaque, fixing them in place with royal icing. Using royal icing, fix the 6 oval plaques to the side of the cake, equally spaced apart, and fix the circle centrally on top of the cake. Fix the ribbon around the edge of the cake board.

MOTHER'S DAY

375 g (13 oz) self-raising flour

1 teaspoon baking powder

5 eggs

325 g (12 oz) soft margarine

275 g (10 oz) caster sugar

75 g (3 oz) ground almonds

½ teaspoon almond essence

grated rind and juice of 3 lemons

1 tablespoon (15 ml) milk

250 g (9 oz) icing sugar, sifted

1.6 kg (3½ lb) ready-to-roll
    fondant icing

cream, green and yellow
    food colouring

1 egg white

YOU WILL ALSO NEED

25 cm (10 inch) petal-shaped
    or round cake tin

30 cm (12 inch) round silver
    cake board

piping gun or bag set

selection of frosted spring flowers

rice paper

1 Grease and line the cake tin. Sift the flour and baking powder into a bowl. Add the eggs, soft margarine, caster sugar, almonds, almond essence, all the lemon rind and the milk. Beat well for 2 minutes, until the mixture is smooth.

2 Turn the mixture into the tin and cook at 160°C (325°F), Gas Mark 3, for 1 hour-1 hour 10 minutes, until the cake feels firm to the touch. Turn out on to a wire rack and leave to cool completely.

3 Place the cake on the board. Mix the lemon juice with 6 tablespoons of the icing sugar. Brush this mixture over the cake and leave until completely absorbed.

4 Colour 1.4 kg (3 lb) of the fondant pale cream and roll out until it is large enough to cover the top and sides of the cake. Lift the fondant over the cake and smooth the sides. Trim around the base.

5 Colour the remaining fondant green and roll a long thin rope to fit around the base of the cake. Roll the remaining green fondant into tiny balls, shaping one side of each ball to form a 'teardrop'.

6 Beat 1 egg white with the remaining icing sugar until smooth. Beat in a few drops of yellow food colouring. Spoon into a piping gun or bag fitted with a plain nozzle and use to secure the 'teardrops' and frosted flowers on top of the cake.

7 Cut out butterfly shapes from rice paper. Secure to the cake with yellow royal icing and pipe an outline around the edges of the wings.

Serves 12

PREPARATION TIME: 45 MINUTES, PLUS OVERNIGHT DRYING

COOKING TIME: 1 HOUR-1 HOUR 10 MINUTES

OVEN TEMPERATURE: 160°C (325°F), GAS MARK 3

TO MAKE FROSTED FLOWERS

Do use: cowslip, freesia, lilac, primrose, rose, violet (these are edible in small quantities)

Don't use: hyacinth, iris, laburnum, lily of the valley, narcissus, snowdrop, tulip

Use only fresh spring flowers: you'll need about 15 flowers. They must be really dry before cutting, or they'll wilt. Cut them 5 mm (¼ inch) down the stem.

Lightly beat 1 egg white with 2 teaspoons of cold water. Sprinkle about 2 tablespoons of caster sugar on to a plate.

Taking each flower in turn, hold by its stem and paint both sides of each petal with the egg white, using a fine, soft paintbrush.

Holding the flower over the plate of caster sugar, sprinkle the flower with sugar, turning to coat evenly. Shake off the excess sugar.

Cover a wire rack with greaseproof paper and make holes in it with a skewer. Poke the stems through the holes. Leave overnight in a warm, dry place.

25TH ANNIVERSARY

1 egg white

1 teaspoon (5 ml) lemon juice

225 g (8 oz) icing sugar, sifted

25 cm (10 inch) round fruit cake,
  covered with almond paste

1.6 kg (3½ lb) ready-to-roll
  fondant icing

snowflake petal dust

50 g (2 oz) caster sugar

silver food paint

YOU WILL ALSO NEED

30 cm (12 inch) round silver
  cake board

5 cm (2 inch) diameter bell mould

leaf cutter

piping gun or bag set

90 cm x 4 cm (36 inches x 1½ inch)
  silver ribbon

1 First make the royal icing: put the egg white, lemon juice and icing sugar in a bowl and beat together until smooth. Cover with damp greaseproof paper.

2 Put the cake on the board. Roll out 1.4 kg (3 lb) of the fondant and cover the cake. Trim the base. Brush the petal dust over the damp icing.

3 Mix the caster sugar with 2-3 drops of water to dampen. Press the sugar mixture firmly into the bell mould. Turn out the sugar bell, as shown below. While damp, carefully slice the bell in half. Position each half on top of the cake and fix with a little royal icing.

4 Roll out the remaining fondant and cut out and mark the leaves. Arrange on the cake and brush with petal dust. From the trimmings, shape the bell hammers and loop. Fix on to the cake.

5 Using a fine plain nozzle, pipe royal icing corn ears, and balls around the base of the cake. Pipe on the numbers. Leave to dry. Paint the bell hammers, loop, corn, numbers and balls with silver food paint. Fix the ribbon with royal icing.

To turn out the sugar bell, tap the top of the mould, then carefully lift away from the bell.

Using royal icing and a fine plain nozzle, pipe ears of corn among the leaves on top of the cake.

Teatime Favourites

COUNTRY PLUM GÂTEAU

1 Grease and line 2 x 20 cm (8 inch) round loose-bottomed sandwich tins.

2 Using an electric whisk, whisk together 3 of the eggs and 75 g (3 oz) of the sugar in a bowl set over a pan of simmering water, until the mixture leaves a trail when the whisk is lifted. Fold in the flour and divide the mixture between the sandwich tins. Place in a preheated oven, 190°C (375°F), Gas Mark 5, for about 12-15 minutes, until well risen. Remove the cakes from the tins and cool on a wire rack.

3 Simmer the plums in a pan with 3 tablespoons (45 ml) apple juice for 12 minutes. Add the remaining sugar and purée until smooth. Reserve 4 tablespoons (60 ml) of the purée and chill the remainder.

4 To make the mousse filling: mix the gelatine with the remaining apple juice and dissolve in a bowl set over a pan of simmering water. Stir the gelatine into the chilled plum purée. Leave to cool slightly.

Whip the double cream until soft peaks form. Separate the remaining 2 eggs and whisk the whites until stiff. Fold the whisked egg whites into the plum purée with the whipped double cream.

5 Line a 20 cm (8 inch) round loose-bottomed deep cake tin with clingfilm. Put one cake in the tin and pour over half the mousse mixture. Top with the remaining cake and mousse. Chill for 3 hours.

6 Lift the gâteau out of the tin and remove the clingfilm. Put the gâteau on a serving plate. Whip the whipping cream until soft peaks form and spread over the top and sides of the cake. Gently press the almonds around the sides of the cake. Drizzle the reserved plum purée over the top.

Serves 8

PREPARATION TIME: 40 MINUTES, PLUS
3 HOURS CHILLING TIME
COOKING TIME: 12-15 MINUTES
OVEN TEMPERATURE: 190°C (375°F),
GAS MARK 5

5 eggs

125 g (5 oz) caster sugar

75 g (3 oz) plain flour, sifted

450 g (1 lb) red plums, quartered, stones removed

142 ml (¼ pint) apple juice

11 g (0.4 oz) sachet gelatine

284 ml (½ pint) double cream

284 ml (½ pint) whipping cream

100 g (4 oz) flaked almonds, toasted

Whisky Dundee Cake

225 g (8 oz) butter, softened

225 g (8 oz) soft light brown sugar

4 eggs, beaten

275 g (10 oz) plain flour, sifted

grated rind and juice of 1 lemon

¼ teaspoon ground cinnamon

1 teaspoon ground mixed spice

100 g (4 oz) whole blanched almonds

50 g (2 oz) mixed candied peel,
   chopped

50 g (2 oz) glacé ginger, roughly
   chopped

325 g (12 oz) mixed dried fruit

2 tablespoons (30 ml) whisky

25 g (1 oz) ground almonds

1   Grease and line a 20 cm (8 inch) round loose-bottomed cake tin.

2   In a large bowl, beat together the butter and brown sugar until pale and fluffy.

3   Beat in the eggs a little at a time, beating well after each addition. Fold in the flour, lemon rind and juice, and the spices.

4   Roughly chop 25 g (1 oz) of the whole almonds. Fold into the cake mixture together with the peel, ginger, dried fruit, whisky and ground almonds. Spoon into the prepared tin and level the surface with the back of a spoon.

5   Arrange the remaining whole almonds in circles on the top of the cake, pressing them in slightly.

6   Cover the cake with a circle of greaseproof paper and place in a preheated oven, 160°C (325°F), Gas Mark 3, for 2¼ hours, until golden or until a skewer inserted into the centre comes out clean. Leave to cool in the tin for 30 minutes, then turn out on to a wire rack and leave to cool completely.

Serves 12

Preparation time: **20 minutes**

Cooking time: 2¼ hours

Oven temperature: 160°C (325°F),
Gas Mark 3

LEMON SANDWICH

225 g (8 oz) butter or margarine,
  softened

225 g (8 oz) caster sugar

4 eggs, beaten

225 g (8 oz) self-raising flour, sifted

1 tablespoon (15 ml) hot water

grated rind and juice of 1 lemon

50 g (2 oz) unsalted butter

100 g (4 oz) icing sugar, sifted

6 tablespoons lemon curd

1 Grease and line 2 x 20 cm (8 inch) round sandwich tins.

2 Beat together the butter and caster sugar until light and fluffy. Beat in the eggs, a little at a time.

3 Fold in the flour, using a metal spoon. Fold in the hot water and lemon rind to produce a soft dropping consistency. Divide the mixture between the prepared tins.

4 Level the surface and place in the centre of a preheated oven, 180°C (350°F), Gas Mark 4, for 40 minutes, or until well risen and golden. Leave to cool in the tins for 5 minutes, then carefully turn out and cool completely on a wire rack.

5 Cream the unsalted butter until pale and fluffy. Beat in the icing sugar and lemon juice. Spread the lemon buttercream over one half of the cake and the lemon curd over the other half.

6 Sandwich the 2 halves together and dust the top of the cake with icing sugar just before serving.

Serves 8

PREPARATION TIME: 30 MINUTES

COOKING TIME: 40 MINUTES

OVEN TEMPERATURE: 180°C (350°F),
GAS MARK 4

JAM SWISS ROLL

3 eggs

90 g (3½ oz) caster sugar

75 g (3 oz) plain flour, sifted

1 tablespoon (15 ml) hot water

5 tablespoons seedless raspberry jam,
*   warmed*

1 Grease and line a 33 x 23 cm (13 x 9 inch) Swiss roll tin.

2 Whisk the eggs with 75 g (3 oz) of the sugar until thick and mousse-like. Lightly fold in the flour and hot water and pour into the tin. Tilt the tin so the mixture spreads evenly.

3 Place in a preheated oven, 200°C (400°F), Gas Mark 6, for 10-12 minutes, until pale golden. Spread a damp tea towel on a work surface and cover it with a piece of greaseproof paper sprinkled with the remaining sugar. Turn the cake out on to the greaseproof paper.

4 Sprinkle the lining paper with 1 tablespoon (15 ml) cold water and peel away. Using a long, sharp knife, trim off the crisp edges, then make an indentation along a short end of the sponge, about 2.5 cm (1 inch) from the edge. Spread the warmed jam evenly over the sponge and roll up from a short side. Cool on a wire rack.

Serves 6

PREPARATION TIME: **10** MINUTES

COOKING TIME: **10-12** MINUTES

OVEN TEMPERATURE: **200**°C (**400**°F),
GAS MARK **6**

STRAWBERRY GÂTEAU

6 eggs

150 g (6 oz) caster sugar

125 g (5 oz) plain flour, sifted

75 g (3 oz) butter, melted

568 ml (1 pint) double cream

450 g (1 lb) strawberries, quartered

1 Grease and line a 23 cm (9 inch) round loose-bottomed cake tin.

2 Whisk the eggs and sugar in a large bowl over a pan of simmering water until the mixture leaves a trail when the whisk is lifted.

3 Remove the bowl from the heat. Using a large metal spoon, fold the flour and melted butter into the egg mixture.

4 Pour the mixture into the prepared tin. Place in a preheated oven, 190°C (375°F), Gas Mark 5, for 10-15 minutes, or until risen and golden and just beginning to shrink away from the sides of the tin.

5 Leave to cool in the tin for 5 minutes, then turn out on to a wire rack and leave to cool completely.

6 Slice the cake into 3 even layers. Whip the cream until soft peaks form. Spread a quarter of the cream over the first layer of cake.

7 Reserve 150 g (6 oz) of the strawberries. Scatter half of the remainder over the layer of cream. Repeat with another layer of cake, a quarter of the cream and 125 g (5 oz) of strawberries. Cover with the third layer of cake and spread with the remaining half of the cream and the reserved strawberries.

Serves 6-10

PREPARATION TIME: 25 MINUTES

COOKING TIME: 10-15 MINUTES

OVEN TEMPERATURE: 190°C (375°F), GAS MARK 5

FRUIT 'N' FIBRE MALT LOAF

100 g (4 oz) high-fibre wheat bran
  breakfast cereal
100 g (4 oz) mixed dried fruit
50 g (2 oz) ready-to-eat dried apricots,
  roughly chopped
275 g (10 oz) demerara sugar
400 ml (14 fl oz) skimmed milk
225 g (8 oz) self-raising flour
1 tablespoon clear honey

1   Put the high-fibre cereal into a large bowl. Add the mixed dried fruit, apricots and all but 1 tablespoon of the demerara sugar. Pour over the skimmed milk and stir until the sugar dissolves. Cover the bowl and leave to stand overnight.

2   Grease and line the base of a 900 g (2 lb) loaf tin. Sift the flour into the soaked fruit mixture and stir until well mixed. Spoon the mixture into the tin and level the surface with the back of a spoon.

3   Place in a preheated oven, 180°C (350°F), Gas Mark 4, for 45 minutes, then cover with foil. Cook for a further 45 minutes, or until a skewer inserted into the centre comes out clean. Leave to cool in the tin for 10 minutes, then turn out on to a wire rack and leave to cool completely.

4   Brush the top of the loaf with honey and sprinkle with the reserved demerara sugar. Serve sliced and spread with butter.

Serves 8

PREPARATION TIME: 10 MINUTES, PLUS OVERNIGHT SOAKING

COOKING TIME: 1½ HOURS

OVEN TEMPERATURE: 180°C (350°F), GAS MARK 4

EASTER TEA RING

500 g (1 lb 2 oz) plain flour
pinch of salt
6 g (¼ oz) sachet fast-action dried yeast
150 g (6 oz) caster sugar
2 eggs, beaten
225 ml (8 fl oz) warm milk
300 g (11 oz) hazelnuts, chopped
65 g (2½ oz) walnuts, chopped
50 g (2 oz) breadcrumbs
6 tablespoons (90 ml) rum
150 g (6 oz) icing sugar
5 glacé cherries, quartered
25 g (1 oz) angelica, cut into strips

1   Sift the flour and salt into a large bowl. Stir in the yeast and 50 g (2 oz) of the caster sugar. Make a well in the centre.

2   Mix the eggs with the warm milk, then add to the dry ingredients. Mix to form a smooth dough, and then shape the dough into a ball and put it in a floured bowl. Cover with an oiled plastic bag and leave to prove in a warm place for 1½ hours or until doubled in size.

3   Meanwhile, mix together the remaining caster sugar, hazelnuts, 50 g (2 oz) of the walnuts, the breadcrumbs and rum.

4   Turn out the risen dough on to a lightly floured surface and knead for 3-4 minutes. Roll out to a 45 x 25 cm (18 x 10 inch) rectangle. Spread the nut mixture over the dough. With the longest edge nearest to you, roll up the dough to form a long sausage shape.

5   Lift on to a greased baking sheet. Join the ends together to form a ring, and seal with a little water. Using scissors, make 8 cuts around the side.

6   Cover and leave to rise for 1 hour. Place in a preheated oven, 180°C (350°F), Gas Mark 4, for 50 minutes. Cool on a wire rack.

7   Mix the icing sugar with 3 tablespoons (45 ml) water; spread over the ring. Decorate with the remaining nuts, cherries and angelica.

Serves 16

PREPARATION TIME: 30 MINUTES, PLUS 2½ HOURS PROVING TIME

COOKING TIME: 50 MINUTES

OVEN TEMPERATURE: 180°C (350°F), GAS MARK 4

ICED BANANA TEA LOAF

75 g (3 oz) butter, softened

150 g (6 oz) soft light brown sugar

2 eggs, beaten

450 g (1 lb) bananas, mashed

200 g (7 oz) self-raising flour, sifted

½ teaspoon bicarbonate of soda

pinch of salt

100 g (4 oz) walnuts, roughly chopped

100 g (4 oz) icing sugar, sifted

1-2 tablespoons (15-30 ml) orange
   juice

25 g (1 oz) honey-coated banana chips

40 g (1½ oz) multi-coloured glacé
   cherries, roughly chopped

1 Grease and line the base of a 900 g (2 lb) loaf tin.

2 Beat together the butter and brown sugar until light and fluffy. Beat in the eggs a little at a time, beating well after each addition.

3 Add the bananas and beat well. Fold in the flour and bicarbonate of soda with the salt and walnuts. Spoon the mixture into the prepared tin and level the surface with the back of a spoon.

4 Place in a preheated oven, 180°C (350°F), Gas Mark 4, for 45 minutes, then cover with foil. Cook for a further 25 minutes, or until well risen and just firm. Turn out and cool on a wire rack.

5 Mix the icing sugar and orange juice to form a smooth icing, and drizzle the icing over the cake. Top with banana chips and cherries.

Serves 8

PREPARATION TIME: 25 MINUTES

COOKING TIME: 1 HOUR 10 MINUTES

OVEN TEMPERATURE: 180°C (350°F), GAS MARK 4

CASHEW AND LEMON CAKE

125 g (5 oz) butter, softened

125 g (5 oz) caster sugar

3 eggs, beaten

150 g (6 oz) self-raising flour, sifted

50 g (2 oz) cornflour, sifted

50 g (2 oz) ground almonds

finely grated rind and juice of 2 lemons

284 ml (½ pint) double cream

1 tablespoon icing sugar, plus extra
   to dust

¼ teaspoon vanilla essence

6 tablespoons lemon curd

75g (3 oz) unsalted cashew nuts,
   toasted and roughly chopped

strips of lemon rind, to decorate

1 Grease and line a 20 cm (8 inch) round deep cake tin.

2 Beat together the butter and caster sugar until light and fluffy. Beat in the eggs a little at a time, beating well after each addition.

3 Stir together the flour, cornflour and ground almonds and fold into the butter mixture with the lemon rind and 1 tablespoon (15 ml) of the lemon juice.

4 Spoon the mixture into the prepared tin and level the surface with the back of a spoon. Place in a pre-heated oven, 180°C (350°F), Gas Mark 4, for 45-50 minutes, until well risen and a skewer inserted into the centre comes out clean. Leave to cool in the tin for about 5 minutes, then turn out on to a wire rack and leave to cool completely.

5 Slice the cake into 3 layers. Whip the cream until soft peaks form. Sift the icing sugar over the whipped cream and gently fold in, together with the vanilla essence.

6 Sandwich the first and second layers of cake together with lemon curd, then place on a serving plate. Spread three-quarters of the whipped cream over the cake and add the top layer.

7 Spread the remaining cream over the top of the cake, then cover with the chopped toasted cashew nuts. Dust with icing sugar and decorate with lemon rind.

Serves 10

PREPARATION TIME: 45 MINUTES

COOKING TIME: 45-50 MINUTES

OVEN TEMPERATURE: 180°C (350°F),

GAS MARK 4

FOREST FRUITS ROULADE

3 eggs

100 g (4 oz) caster sugar

100 g (4 oz) plain flour

1 tablespoon (15 ml) hot water

340 ml (12 fl oz) whipping cream

25 g (1 oz) icing sugar, sifted

50 g (2 oz) each blueberries,
*   raspberries and redcurrants*

sprigs of mint, to decorate

1 Grease and line a 33 x 23 cm (13 x 9 inch) Swiss roll tin.

2 Whisk together the eggs and caster sugar in a large bowl set over a pan of simmering water until thick and mousse-like. Remove from the heat and continue whisking until the mixture is cool. Sift in the flour, add the hot water and fold together, using a metal spoon.

3 Pour the mixture into the tin, tilting gently until the mixture fills the tin evenly. Place in a preheated oven, 220°C (425°F), Gas Mark 7, for 8-10 minutes, until golden.

4 Turn out on to a sheet of nonstick baking paper and remove the lining paper. Trim the edges of the cake with a sharp knife and carefully roll up with the nonstick paper on the inside. Cool on a wire rack.

5 Whip the cream until soft peaks form, then fold in the icing sugar. Put half into a clean bowl. Roughly chop half the fruit and stir into half the cream.

6 Unroll the cake and spread with the fruit cream. Roll up and lift on to a serving plate. Spread the remaining cream over the cake and decorate with the remaining fruit and mint sprigs.

Serves 8

PREPARATION TIME: **20 MINUTES**

COOKING TIME: **8-10 MINUTES**

OVEN TEMPERATURE: **220°C (425°F), GAS MARK 7**

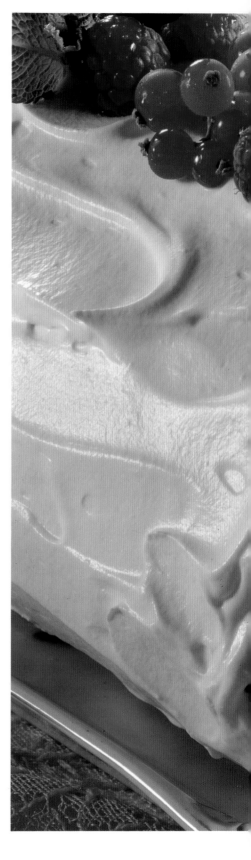

ICED MARBLE CAKE

150 g (6 oz) butter

150 g (6 oz) caster sugar

3 eggs, beaten

150 g (6 oz) self-raising flour, sifted

1 tablespoon cocoa powder, sifted

75 g (3 oz) milk chocolate drops

1 tablespoon (15 ml) milk

75 g (3 oz) glacé cherries, quartered

few drops of red food colouring

grated rind and juice of 1 lemon

100 g (4 oz) icing sugar

15 g (½ oz) flaked almonds

1   Grease and line an 18 cm (7 inch) round, deep, loose-bottomed cake tin.

2   Beat the butter and caster sugar until light and fluffy. Gradually beat in the eggs, adding a little flour if the mixture begins to curdle. Fold in the remaining flour, and divide the mixture between 3 bowls.

3   Beat the cocoa, 50 g (2 oz) of the chocolate drops and the milk into 1 of the bowls. Roughly chop 50 g (2 oz) of the cherries and fold into the second bowl, with the red food colouring. Add the rind and 1 tablespoon (15 ml) of the lemon juice to the remaining bowl of cake mixture.

4   Spoon tablespoons of the 3 cake mixtures randomly into the prepared tin. Level the surface and place in a preheated oven, 180°F (350°F), Gas Mark 4, for 1 hour, until well risen and golden brown. Turn out and cool on a wire rack.

5   Mix the icing sugar with enough of the remaining lemon juice to make a thick, smooth icing. Spread over the top of the cake, then scatter the cake with flaked almonds and the remaining cherries. Melt the remaining chocolate drops and drizzle over the cake. Leave to set for about 15 minutes.

Serves 8

PREPARATION TIME: 25 MINUTES, PLUS 15 MINUTES SETTING TIME

COOKING TIME: 1 HOUR

OVEN TEMPERATURE: 180°C (350°F), GAS MARK 4

GLACÉ ALMOND MADEIRA

215 g (7½ oz) self-raising flour

40 g (1½ oz) ground almonds

25 g (1 oz) cornflour

pinch of salt

275 g (10 oz) butter

275 g (10 oz) caster sugar

½ teaspoon (2.5 ml) almond essence

5 eggs, beaten

1½ tablespoons (22.5 ml) milk

1 tablespoon apricot jam

1 tablespoon (15 ml) orange juice

100 g (4 oz) assorted glacé fruit, very
   thinly sliced

1 Grease and line a 900 g (2 lb) loaf tin.

2 Sift the flour, ground almonds and cornflour into a large bowl, then stir in a pinch of salt.

3 In a separate bowl, beat together the butter, sugar and almond essence until light and fluffy. Add the eggs a little at a time, beating well after each addition, and adding the milk and a little of the flour mixture to prevent curdling. Gently fold the flour mixture into the egg mixture until smooth.

4 Spoon the mixture into the prepared loaf tin. Make a dip in the centre with the back of a spoon and place in a preheated oven, 180°C (350°F), Gas Mark 4, for 1 hour 20-25 minutes, or until well risen and a skewer inserted into the centre comes out clean. Turn out and cool on a wire rack.

5 Heat the apricot jam and orange juice together until the jam has melted. Brush over the cake and arrange the glacé fruit on top.

Serves 8

PREPARATION TIME: **20** MINUTES

COOKING TIME: **1** HOUR **20-25**
MINUTES

OVEN TEMPERATURE: 180°C (350°F),
GAS MARK **4**

UPSIDE-DOWN PEAR CAKE

25 g (1 oz) demerara sugar

822 g (1 lb 12 oz) can pear halves in syrup, drained, syrup reserved

75 g (3 oz) glacé cherries, halved

225 g (8 oz) butter, softened

225 g (8 oz) caster sugar

4 eggs, beaten

225 g (8 oz) self-raising flour, sifted

100 g (4 oz) walnuts, chopped

2 tablespoons (30 ml) milk

3 tablespoons (45 ml) maple syrup

1 Grease and line a 20 cm (8 inch) round, deep, loose-bottomed tin.

2 Sprinkle the demerara sugar over the base of the tin. Pat the pears dry on kitchen paper. Put a cherry half in the hollowed core of 8 pear halves. Arrange, rounded side up, in the base of the tin.

3 Beat together the butter and caster sugar until light and fluffy. Beat in the eggs, a little at a time, beating well after each addition. Toss the remaining cherry halves in flour and then fold into the creamed mixture with the flour, walnuts and milk.

4 Spoon the mixture into the cake tin. Level the surface and place on the top shelf of a preheated oven, 180°C (350°F), Gas Mark 4, for 1¼ hours, or until a skewer inserted into the centre comes out clean. Cover the top with foil if the cake is over-browning during cooking. Cool in the tin for 10 minutes.

5 Meanwhile, put 225 ml (8 fl oz) of the reserved pear syrup and the maple syrup in a saucepan. Bring to the boil and simmer for 10 minutes or until reduced by half.

6 Turn the cake on to a plate and drizzle over the hot syrup.

Serves 8

PREPARATION TIME: 25 MINUTES

COOKING TIME: 1 HOUR 25 MINUTES

OVEN TEMPERATURE: 180°C (350°F), GAS MARK 4

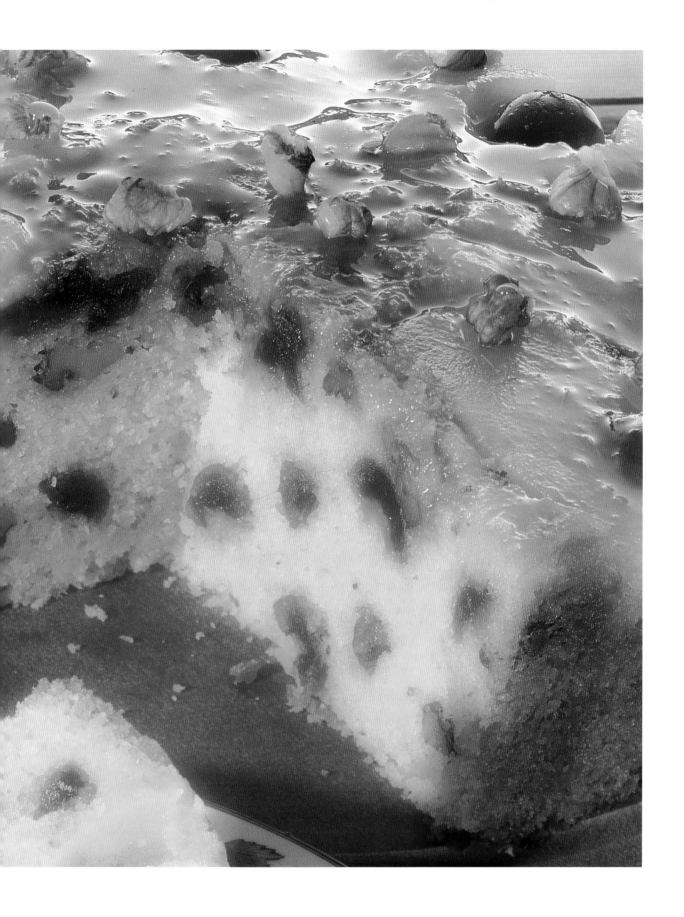

Vienna Slice

275 g (10 oz) shortcrust pastry

411 g (14 oz) jar of mincemeat

150 g (6 oz) butter

100 g (4 oz) caster sugar

3 eggs

few drops of vanilla essence

225 g (8 oz) plain flour, sifted

8 glacé cherries, quartered

strips of angelica, chopped

icing sugar, to dust

1 Roll out the pastry on a lightly floured surface until it is large enough to fit a 30 x 11 cm (12 x 4½ inch) loose-bottomed flan tin. Alternatively, roll it out to line a 20 cm (8 inch) round flan ring. Chill for 15 minutes.

2 Line with greaseproof paper, fill with baking beans and bake blind in a preheated oven, 190°C (375°F), Gas Mark 5, for 10 minutes. Remove the baking beans and cook the pastry for a further 5 minutes. Remove from the oven and leave to cool.

3 Spoon in the mincemeat and level the surface. Set aside.

4 Cream together the butter and caster sugar. Separate 2 eggs; beat 2 yolks, 1 whole egg and the vanilla essence into the creamed mixture. Beat in the flour, until smooth. Spoon into a piping bag fitted with a large star nozzle and pipe a lattice on top of the mincemeat. Pipe rosettes in between the lattice. Chill for 1 hour.

5 Decorate with glacé cherries and angelica, and then bake for 25-30 minutes, until golden. Cool on a wire rack. Dust with icing sugar.

Serves 8

Preparation time: 20 minutes, plus 1¼ hours chilling time

Cooking time: 40-45 minutes

Oven temperature: 190°C (375°F), Gas Mark 5

ORANGE MARMALADE LOAF

3 oranges

3 eggs

150 g (6 oz) butter or soft margarine

150 g (6 oz) soft brown sugar

275 g (10 oz) self-raising flour

1 teaspoon ground mixed spice

4 tablespoons coarse-cut marmalade

100 g (4 oz) walnut pieces

75 g (3 oz) mixed dried fruit

4 glacé cherries, quartered

1 Grease and line the base of a 900 g (2 lb) loaf tin.

2 Squeeze the juice from 1 orange and put it in a food processor with the eggs, butter or margarine, sugar, flour, spice and 2 tablespoons of the marmalade. Process the mixture for 1 minute.

3 Remove the mixing bowl from the food processor and then stir in the walnut pieces and dried fruit. Spoon the mixture into the prepared loaf tin and level the surface, using a spatula.

4 Place in a preheated oven, 160°C (325°F), Gas Mark 3, for 45 minutes, then cover with foil to prevent burning. Cook the cake for a further 30 minutes, or until it is well risen and a skewer inserted into the centre comes out clean. Turn out and cool on a wire rack.

5 Rub the remaining marmalade through a sieve into a small saucepan and discard the peel. Add 2 tablespoons (30 ml) of water and gently melt the marmalade over a low heat to make a glaze.

6 Using a sharp knife, peel and thinly slice the remaining oranges, remove any pips and poach in the marmalade mixture for 2-3 minutes. Remove the orange slices and set aside.

7 Brush half the marmalade glaze over the cake. Arrange the orange slices on top of the cake, overlapping slightly, and brush with the remaining glaze. Decorate with the glacé cherry quarters.

Serves 10

PREPARATION TIME: 20 MINUTES

COOKING TIME: 1 HOUR 20 MINUTES

OVEN TEMPERATURE: 160°C (325°F), GAS MARK 3

PINEAPPLE AND GINGER CAKE

265 g (9½ oz) plain flour, sifted

3 teaspoons baking powder

4 teaspoons ground ginger

75 g (3 oz) butter, softened

75 g (3 oz) soft light brown sugar

3 eggs, beaten

2 tablespoons (30 ml) black treacle

3 tablespoons (45 ml) golden syrup

2 teaspoons bicarbonate of soda

115 ml (4 fl oz) ginger beer

75 g (3 oz) bottled stem ginger, drained
and chopped, plus 1 tablespoon
(15 ml) syrup from the ginger bottle

75 g (3 oz) glacé pineapple, chopped

2 tablespoons pineapple conserve

1 Grease and line an 18 cm (7 inch) round deep cake tin.

2 Sift together 250 g (9 oz) of the flour, the baking powder and the ground ginger.

3 Beat together the butter and brown sugar until light and fluffy. Gradually add the eggs, a little at a time, beating well after each addition. If the mixture begins to curdle, add 2 tablespoons of the flour mixture and continue beating.

4 In a small saucepan, heat the black treacle and golden syrup until they have melted. Add to the egg mixture with the bicarbonate of soda and ginger beer. Beat to a smooth batter.

5 Make a well in the centre of the flour mixture and gradually beat in the batter until smooth.

6 Toss the stem ginger and glacé pineapple in the reserved flour and gently fold into the batter. Spoon into the prepared tin and place in a preheated oven, 160°C (325°F), Gas Mark 3, for 20 minutes.

7 Remove the cake from the oven. Drop teaspoons of the pineapple conserve evenly over the cake. Return the cake to the oven and cook for a further 35 minutes, until well risen and a skewer inserted into the centre comes out clean. Turn out on to a wire rack and brush with the ginger syrup. Leave to cool completely before cutting.

Serves 12

PREPARATION TIME: 20 MINUTES

COOKING TIME: 55 MINUTES

OVEN TEMPERATURE: 160°C (325°F),
GAS MARK 3

Small Cakes

MANDARIN PECAN SLICES

1 Grease and line a 30 x 20 cm (12 x 8 inch) Swiss roll tin.

2 Stir together 325 g (12 oz) of the flour, 225 g (8 oz) of the sugar and the baking powder.

3 Melt 50 g (2 oz) of the butter and stir in the eggs and milk. Pour the liquid into the flour mixture and stir until smooth. Do not beat.

4 Fold the mandarins, pecan nuts and grated orange rind into the cake mixture. Pour the mixture into the prepared tin.

5 Rub together the reserved flour, sugar, butter and the cinnamon, and sprinkle over the cake mixture. Place in a preheated oven, 180°C (350°F), Gas Mark 4, for 40 minutes, until golden or until a skewer inserted into the centre comes out clean. Leave to cool in the tin, and then slice into 16 pieces.

Makes 16

PREPARATION TIME: **20** MINUTES

COOKING TIME: **40** MINUTES

OVEN TEMPERATURE: 180°C (350°F),

GAS MARK 4

375 g (13 oz) plain flour, sifted

250 g (9 oz) caster sugar

3 teaspoons baking powder

75 g (3 oz) butter

2 eggs, beaten

170 ml (6 fl oz) milk

198 g (7 oz) can mandarins in natural juice, drained and roughly chopped

100 g (4 oz) pecan nuts, roughly chopped

finely grated rind of 2 oranges

2 teaspoons ground cinnamon

DEVONSHIRE SPLITS

450 g (1 lb) plain flour

½ teaspoon salt

6 g (¼ oz) sachet fast-action dried yeast

25 g (1 oz) caster sugar

50 g (2 oz) butter, melted

284 ml (½ pint) semi-skimmed milk,
    warmed

284 ml (½ pint) double cream

225 g (8 oz) raspberry jam, sieved

15 g (½ oz) icing sugar, sifted

1 Sift the flour and salt into a large bowl. Stir in the yeast and caster sugar. Make a well in the centre.

2 Stir together the melted butter and milk, then add to the flour mixture. Mix to form a soft dough.

3 Turn the dough out on to a lightly floured surface and knead by hand for 5 minutes, until smooth and elastic. Place in a clean bowl, cover with a damp cloth and leave to prove in a warm place for 1 hour or until doubled in size.

4 Turn the proved dough out on to a lightly floured surface and divide it into 12 pieces; knead each piece for 1 minute. Shape into rounds and place on 2 greased baking sheets, spaced well apart. Brush off any excess flour. Cover with oiled cling-film and leave in a warm place for 30 minutes or until doubled in size.

5 Place on the middle shelf of a preheated oven, 220°C (425°F), Gas Mark 7, for 15 minutes, until well risen and golden. Cool on a wire rack.

6 Split the buns open. Whip the cream until soft peaks form. Fill the buns with cream and sieved jam, and sift the icing sugar over the top.

Makes 12

PREPARATION TIME: 30 MINUTES, PLUS 1½ HOURS PROVING TIME

COOKING TIME: 15 MINUTES

OVEN TEMPERATURE: 220°C (425°F), GAS MARK 7

FAIRY CAKES

150 g (6 oz) butter, softened

150 g (6 oz) caster sugar

3 eggs, beaten

150 g (6 oz) self-raising flour, sifted

grated rind and juice of 1 orange

225 g (8 oz) icing sugar, sifted

50 g (2 oz) ready-to-roll fondant icing

orange and yellow food colouring

1 Line 2 x 12-hole cake tins with paper cake cases.

2 Beat together the butter and caster sugar until light and fluffy. Add the beaten eggs to the butter and sugar mixture, a little at a time, beating well after each addition.

3 Fold in the flour, using a large metal spoon. Stir in the grated orange rind. Reserve 2 tablespoons of the juice and add the remainder to the cake mixture.

4 Spoon the mixture into the paper cake cases to come within 1 cm (½ inch) of the top. Place in a preheated oven, 180°C (350°F), Gas Mark 4, for 15 minutes, until well risen and golden. Remove the cakes from the tins and cool on a wire rack.

5 Beat together the icing sugar, the reserved orange juice and a few drops of water to form a smooth, thick icing. Spread 2 teaspoons of icing on top of each cake.

6 Colour half of the fondant orange and half yellow. Roll out each piece thinly on a surface lightly dusted with icing sugar. Using a small flower cutter, stamp out orange and yellow flowers. Arrange the flowers in alternate colours in a circle on top of each cake. Leave to dry for 1 hour.

Makes 24

PREPARATION TIME: 1 HOUR, PLUS

1 HOUR DRYING TIME

COOKING TIME: 15 MINUTES

OVEN TEMPERATURE: 180°C (350°F),

GAS MARK 4

STRAWBERRY TARTLETS

225 ml (8 fl oz) milk

1 vanilla pod or ½ teaspoon vanilla
   essence

2 egg yolks, plus 1 whole egg, beaten,
   to glaze

50 g (2 oz) caster sugar

1 tablespoon plain flour, sifted

450 g (1 lb) puff pastry, thawed
   if frozen

450 g (1 lb) fresh strawberries, halved
   lengthways

3 tablespoons redcurrant jelly

1 Place the milk in a saucepan with the vanilla pod or essence, and bring to the boil. Remove the pan from the heat and leave to stand for 20 minutes. Remove the vanilla pod, if using (pat dry and store for future use).

2 Whisk together the 2 egg yolks and all but 1 teaspoon of the caster sugar until pale and thick, so that the mixture leaves a trail when the whisk is lifted. Whisk in the flour.

3 Gradually whisk the vanilla-flavoured milk into the egg mixture and then return it to the saucepan. Place over a low heat and stir constantly for 10 minutes, until the custard thickens. Sprinkle the surface of the custard with the reserved sugar to prevent a skin forming. Leave to cool.

4 On a lightly floured surface, roll out the pastry to a thickness of 5 mm (¼ inch). Using a 9 cm (3½ inch) cutter or a small saucer as a guide, cut out 8 circles.

5 Using a 7 cm (3 inch) cutter, mark a circle 1 cm (½ inch) from the edge of each pastry circle. Knock up the edge of each circle with the tip of a sharp knife.

6 Brush the pastry circles with beaten egg to glaze, and place in a preheated oven, 230°C (450°F), Gas Mark 8, for 15 minutes, until well risen and golden brown. Cool on a wire rack.

7 Run a knife around the inner circle and press down gently to make a small dip. Spoon some of the custard into each tartlet and arrange the strawberries on top.

8 Warm the redcurrant jelly in a small pan over a low heat and brush over the strawberries. Serve with cream, if liked.

Makes 8

PREPARATION TIME: 25 MINUTES, PLUS
20 MINUTES STANDING TIME

COOKING TIME: 25 MINUTES

OVEN TEMPERATURE: 230°C (450°F),
GAS MARK 8

FONDANT FANCIES

50 g (2 oz) butter, softened

4 tablespoons clear honey

150 g (6 oz) plain flour, sifted

2 teaspoons baking powder, sifted

3 tablespoons ground ginger

1 teaspoon bicarbonate of soda

200 ml (7 fl oz) milk

2 eggs, beaten

675 g (1½ lb) icing sugar, sifted

yellow food colouring

50 g (2 oz) ready-to-roll fondant icing

peach food colouring

silver dragées

yellow mimosa balls

thin satin ribbon (optional)

1 Grease and line an 18 cm (7 inch) square deep cake tin.

2 Beat together the butter and honey until light and fluffy. Beat in the flour, baking powder, ginger, bicarbonate of soda, milk and eggs.

3 Spoon the mixture into the prepared tin. Place in a preheated oven, 160°C (325°F), Gas Mark 3, for 45 minutes, until well risen.

4 Cool in the tin, and then turn on to a board and cut into 6 squares.

5 Place the icing sugar in a bowl and add enough water to make a very thick, smooth icing. Transfer half the icing to another bowl and colour it yellow. Cover the white icing with clingfilm to prevent a crust forming.

6 Push a fork into the base of a cake to hold it while you spoon some of the icing over. Smooth the icing carefully, using a warm knife, then set the cake on a wire rack. Cover the remaining cakes in the same way, reserving a little icing.

7 Colour half of the fondant yellow and half peach. Roll out and shape into flowers; fill the centres of the flowers with dragées or mimosa balls. Attach the flowers (and ribbon, if using) to the cakes with the reserved icing.

Makes 6

PREPARATION TIME: 40 MINUTES

COOKING TIME: 45 MINUTES

OVEN TEMPERATURE: 160°C (325°F), GAS MARK 3

CREAM SCONES

325 g (12 oz) self-raising flour

½ teaspoon salt

1½ teaspoons baking powder

1½ teaspoons caster sugar

75 g (3 oz) butter, cubed

215 ml (7½ fl oz) milk

few drops of vanilla essence

1 egg, beaten

284 ml (½ pint) whipping cream

1 tablespoon icing sugar, sifted, plus
*   extra to dust*

1   Heat a baking sheet in the oven at 230°C (450°F), Gas Mark 8. Sift together the flour, salt, baking powder and caster sugar.

2   Rub in the butter until the mixture resembles fine breadcrumbs. Add the milk and vanilla essence and mix to form a soft dough.

3   Roll out to a thickness of 1.5 cm (³/₄ inch) and stamp out 9 x 6 cm (2½ inch) rounds. Reroll the trimmings and stamp out further rounds. Place on the hot baking sheet, brush with egg and bake in the hot oven for 8-10 minutes. Cool on a wire rack.

4   Whip the cream until soft peaks form and fold in the icing sugar. Split the scones and fill with the cream. If liked, decorate with strawberries and dust with icing sugar.

Makes 12

PREPARATION TIME: 15 MINUTES

COOKING TIME: 8-10 MINUTES

OVEN TEMPERATURE: 230°C (450°F), GAS MARK 8

MILLE-FEUILLES

450 g (1 lb) puff pastry, thawed if frozen

2 tablespoons (30 ml) milk

284 ml (½ pint) double cream

2 teaspoons (10 ml) rosewater

100 g (4 oz) icing sugar, sifted

225 g (8 oz) strawberries, sliced

1   On a lightly floured surface, roll out the puff pastry to a thickness of 5 mm (¼ inch) to form a rectangle measuring 30 x 20 cm (12 x 8 inches). Cut into 12 rectangles and place on 2 baking sheets.

2   Brush the rectangles with milk and place in a preheated oven, 220°C (425°F), Gas Mark 7, for 8-10 minutes. Cool on a wire rack, then carefully split each pastry rectangle horizontally into 3 layers.

3   Whip together the cream and rosewater with 50 g (2 oz) of the icing sugar until soft peaks form. Sandwich the pastry layers together with cream and sliced strawberries.

4   Mix the remaining icing sugar with enough cold water to form a paste, and drizzle over the pastries.

Makes 12

PREPARATION TIME: 20 MINUTES

COOKING TIME: 8-10 MINUTES

OVEN TEMPERATURE: 220°C (425°F), GAS MARK 7

CHOCOLATE SQUARES

100 g (4 oz) cocoa powder, sifted

485 ml (17 fl oz) boiling water

200 g (7 oz) butter, softened

475 g (17 oz) granulated sugar

325 g (12 oz) plain flour, sifted

1 teaspoon bicarbonate of soda

½ teaspoon baking powder

3 eggs, beaten

40 g (1½ oz) plain chocolate, melted

40 g (1½ oz) white chocolate, melted

1 Grease and line a 20 cm (8 inch) square cake tin.

2 Mix the cocoa with the boiling water and stir until smooth. Leave to cool.

3 Beat together the butter and sugar until light. In a separate bowl, sift together the flour, bicarbonate of soda and baking powder.

4 Gradually beat the eggs into the butter and sugar mixture, beating well after each addition and alternately beating in a little flour. Beat well. Fold in the cocoa mixture and the remaining flour.

5 Pour the cake mixture into the prepared tin and place in a pre-heated oven, 180°C (350°F), Gas Mark 4, for 1 hour 40 minutes or until a skewer inserted into the centre of the cake comes out clean. Leave to cool in the tin for 10 minutes, then turn out and cool upside down on a wire rack. Trim the surface of the cake level and then cut into 16 squares.

6 Put the melted plain chocolate into a piping bag with a fine nozzle and drizzle over the squares. Repeat with the melted white chocolate, piping at right angles to the plain chocolate. Leave to set.

Makes 16

PREPARATION TIME: 20 MINUTES

COOKING TIME: 1 HOUR 40 MINUTES

OVEN TEMPERATURE: 180°C

(350°F), GAS MARK 4

HOT CROSS BUNS

450 g (1 lb) strong plain flour, sifted

6 g (¼ oz) sachet fast-action dried yeast

1 teaspoon salt

1 teaspoon ground mixed spice

1 teaspoon ground cinnamon

½ teaspoon grated nutmeg

75 g (3 oz) caster sugar

50 g (2 oz) butter, finely cubed

125 g (5 oz) mixed dried fruit

310 ml (11 fl oz) hand-hot milk

1 egg, beaten

50 g (2 oz) shortcrust pastry

1 Stir together the flour, yeast, salt, spices and 50 g (2 oz) of the sugar. Rub in the butter until the mixture resembles fine bread-crumbs, then stir in the dried fruit.

2 Beat 284 ml (10 fl oz) of the milk and the egg into the flour mixture to form a soft, sticky dough. Turn out on to a lightly floured surface and knead for 10 minutes, until the dough is smooth, elastic and no longer sticky. Place in a clean bowl, cover with oiled clingfilm, and leave to prove in a warm place for 1 hour or until doubled in size.

3 Turn out on to a lightly floured surface and knead for 2-3 minutes. Divide the dough into 12 pieces and then shape into rounds. Place on 2 greased baking sheets, cover with oiled clingfilm and leave to prove in a warm place for 30 minutes or until doubled in size.

4 Roll out the pastry and cut into narrow strips about 7 cm (3 inches) long. Dampen the strips and criss-cross over the buns.

5 Place in a preheated oven, 190°C (375°F), Gas Mark 5, for 16-20 minutes, until risen and golden.

6 To glaze the buns: gently heat the remaining sugar and milk with 2 tablespoons (30 ml) water until the sugar has melted. Brush the hot buns twice with the glaze.

Makes 12

PREPARATION TIME: **20 MINUTES**,
PLUS 1½ HOURS PROVING TIME
COOKING TIME: **16-20 MINUTES**
OVEN TEMPERATURE: **190°C (375°F)**,
GAS MARK 5

CHELSEA BUNS

450 g (1 lb) strong plain flour, sifted

½ teaspoon salt

½ teaspoon ground mixed spice

50 g (2 oz) butter

6 g (¼ oz) sachet fast-action dried yeast

270 ml (9½ fl oz) hand-hot milk

1 egg, beaten

100 g (4 oz) luxury mixed dried fruit

50 g (2 oz) soft light brown sugar

½ teaspoon ground cinnamon

2 tablespoons clear honey, warmed

1 Grease and line the base of a 30 cm (12 inch) square cake tin.

2 Sift the flour, salt and mixed spice into a bowl. Rub in half the butter. Add the yeast and stir well.

3 Beat 255 ml (9 fl oz) of the milk with the egg and, using a round-bladed knife, stir into the dry ingredients to form a dough that leaves the sides of the bowl clean. Turn out on to a lightly floured surface and knead for 5 minutes, until smooth. Place in a clean, lightly oiled bowl, cover with oiled clingfilm and leave to prove in a warm place for 1 hour or until doubled in size.

4 Turn out on to a lightly floured surface. Knead lightly and roll out to form a 30 x 23 cm (12 x 9 inch) rectangle. Melt the remaining butter and brush over the dough. Sprinkle over the dried fruit, sugar and cinnamon and roll up loosely, lengthways. Using a sharp knife, trim and cut into 9 rounds. Place in the prepared tin and prove for 1 hour or until doubled in size.

5 Brush with the remaining milk and place in a preheated oven, 190°C (375°F), Gas Mark 5, for 30 minutes, until golden brown. Lift on to a wire rack and drizzle over the honey. Cool for 5 minutes.

Makes 9

PREPARATION TIME: 45 MINUTES, PLUS 2 HOURS PROVING TIME

COOKING TIME: 30 MINUTES

OVEN TEMPERATURE: 190°C (375°F), GAS MARK 5

RASPBERRY DOUGHNUTS

225 g (8 oz) plain flour, sifted

¼ teaspoon salt

6 g (¼ oz) sachet fast-action dried yeast

65 g (2½ oz) caster sugar

15 g (½ oz) butter

1 egg, beaten

4 tablespoons (60 ml) warm milk

16 raspberries

8 teaspoons seedless raspberry jam

1 teaspoon ground cinnamon

sunflower or groundnut oil for
    deep-fat frying

1 Place the flour, salt, yeast and 15 g (½ oz) each of sugar and butter in a large bowl. Rub in the butter and make a well in the centre.

2 Beat together the egg and warm milk, and then stir into the dry ingredients to form an elastic and slightly sticky dough. Turn out on to a lightly floured surface and knead for 2 minutes or until smooth. Place in a clean, lightly oiled bowl, cover with a damp tea towel and leave to prove in a warm place for 1 hour or until doubled in size.

3 Turn out the dough and divide into 8 pieces. Knead each piece lightly and roll into a ball. Pat the balls into 7 cm (3 inch) rounds. Put 2 raspberries and 1 teaspoon of jam in the centre of each round and then pinch the edges together to seal. Place on a lightly floured baking sheet, rounded side uppermost. Cover lightly with clingfilm and leave to prove in a warm place for a further 10 minutes.

4 In a small bowl, stir together the remaining sugar and cinnamon. Heat the oil in a deep-fat fryer until a cube of bread rises, sizzling gently. The oil should not be bubbling.

5 Cook the doughnuts 2 at a time. Carefully lower them into the hot oil and fry for 5 minutes, turning once, until puffed up and golden. Remove and drain on kitchen paper. Roll the doughnuts in the cinnamon sugar while still warm.

Note: to test if the doughnuts are cooked, make a cut in the first doughnut. If the dough is wet and stringy, reduce the oil temperature and cook for a further 1 minute.

Makes 8

PREPARATION TIME: 25 MINUTES, plus 1 HOUR 10 MINUTES PROVING TIME

COOKING TIME: 20 MINUTES

RASPBERRY MERINGUES

2 egg whites

150 g (6 oz) caster sugar

426 ml (¾ pint) whipping cream

225 g (8 oz) raspberries, thawed if
    frozen

1 Line 2 baking sheets with greaseproof paper.

2 Place the egg whites in a clean, oil-free bowl and whisk until stiff. Whisk in the sugar, 1 tablespoon at a time, until smooth and glossy.

3 Put 16 spoonfuls of the mixture on to the 2 baking sheets. Place in a preheated oven, 110°C (225°F), Gas Mark ¼, for 1¾ hours or until crisp. Carefully lift them off the baking sheets and cool on a wire rack.

4 Whip the cream until soft peaks form, fold in the raspberries and use to sandwich the meringues.

Makes 8

PREPARATION TIME: 15 MINUTES

COOKING TIME: 1¾ HOURS

OVEN TEMPERATURE: 110°C (225°F), GAS MARK ¼

MOCHA CREAM ECLAIRS

50 g (2 oz) butter

65 g (2½ oz) plain flour, sifted

2 eggs, lightly beaten

150 g (6 oz) icing sugar, sifted

1 tablespoon (15 ml) coffee and
*   chicory essence*

284 ml (½ pint) double cream

50 g (2 oz) plain chocolate

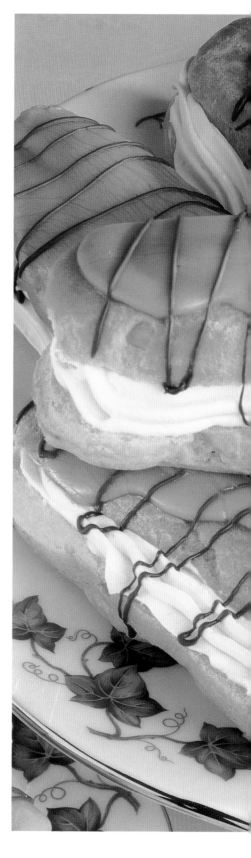

1 Put the butter into a saucepan with 142 ml (¼ pint) cold water and bring to the boil. Remove from the heat and add the sifted flour, all at once. Beat until smooth and the paste forms a ball. Leave to cool for 2 minutes.

2 Gradually add the eggs, beating well after each addition, until the paste is glossy. Spoon into a piping bag fitted with a large plain nozzle.

3 Pipe 8 x 10 cm (4 inch) lengths of the choux paste on to a large greased baking sheet, spaced well apart. Place in a preheated oven, 220°C (425°F), Gas Mark 7, for 12 minutes, until risen and golden. Pierce the bases to allow the steam to escape. Cool on a wire rack.

4 Stir together the icing sugar, coffee essence and enough water to make a smooth icing. Slit each éclair in half and dip the tops in the icing. Leave to set on a wire rack.

5 Whip the cream until soft peaks form and, using a large star nozzle, pipe the cream on to each éclair base. Cover with the iced tops.

6 Melt the chocolate, spoon into a piping bag fitted with a fine nozzle and drizzle over the éclairs. Leave to set.

Makes 8

PREPARATION TIME: 30 MINUTES

COOKING TIME: 12 MINUTES

OVEN TEMPERATURE: 220°C (425°F),
GAS MARK 7

SPICY HOT CROSS MUFFINS

400 g (14 oz) plain flour

200 g (7 oz) caster sugar

1½ tablespoons baking powder

½ teaspoon salt

1 teaspoon ground mixed spice

150 g (6 oz) butter, cubed

100 g (4 oz) currants

100 g (4 oz) mixed peel

1 egg and 1 egg yolk, beaten together

284 ml (½ pint) milk

50 g (2 oz) shortcrust pastry

2 tablespoons clear honey, warmed

1 Grease and line the bases of 9 muffin tins.

2 Mix together the flour, sugar, baking powder, salt and spice in a large bowl. Rub in the butter until the mixture resembles fine bread-crumbs. Stir in the currants and 50 g (2 oz) of the mixed peel.

3 Beat the egg and egg yolk with 225 ml (8 fl oz) of the milk, and then beat into the dry ingredients until the mixture is smooth.

4 Divide the mixture between the prepared tins, set on a baking sheet and place in a preheated oven, 200°C (400°F), Gas Mark 6, for 15 minutes, until the muffins are risen and just beginning to brown.

5 Meanwhile, roll out the pastry on a lightly floured surface and cut into 18 strips, each measuring 7 cm x 5 mm (3 inches x ¼ inch).

6 Brush the muffins with the remaining milk and crisscross 2 pastry strips on each muffin. Cook for a further 15 minutes.

7 Brush the tops of the muffins with the honey and sprinkle with the remaining mixed peel. Leave to cool in the tins for 5 minutes, then run a knife around the edges and turn out. Serve warm.

Makes 9

PREPARATION TIME: **20** MINUTES

COOKING TIME: **30** MINUTES

OVEN TEMPERATURE: **200°C (400°F)**,
GAS MARK **6**

More Muffins

COURGETTE AND CHERRY

350 g (12½ oz) plain flour

290 g (10½ oz) caster sugar

40 g (1½ oz) porridge oats

1 tablespoon baking powder

1 teaspoon salt

1 teaspoon ground cinnamon

100 g (4 oz) mixed nuts, chopped

4 eggs, beaten

225 g (8 oz) courgettes, grated

170 ml (6 fl oz) sunflower oil

50 g (2 oz) glacé cherries, chopped

demerara sugar, to sprinkle

1 Grease and line the bases of 9 muffin tins.

2 Mix together the flour, caster sugar, oats, baking powder, salt and cinnamon. Stir in the remaining ingredients and beat well.

3 Divide the mixture between the prepared muffin tins, set on a baking sheet and place in a preheated oven, 200°C (400°F), Gas Mark 6, for 25-30 minutes, until risen and a skewer inserted into the centre comes out clean. Sprinkle with demerara sugar and serve warm.

Makes 9

PREPARATION TIME: 15 MINUTES

COOKING TIME: 25-30 MINUTES

OVEN TEMPERATURE: 200°C (400°F), GAS MARK 6

BRAN AND MAPLE SYRUP

375 g (13 oz) bran flakes, finely crushed

225 g (8 oz) plain flour

2 teaspoons bicarbonate of soda

½ teaspoon salt

2 eggs, beaten

284 ml (½ pint) buttermilk

115 ml (4 fl oz) maple syrup

85 ml (3 fl oz) sunflower oil

115 ml (4 fl oz) milk

2 tablespoons clear honey, warmed

50 g (2 oz) flaked almonds, toasted

1 Grease and line the bases of 9 muffin tins.

2 Mix the bran flakes, flour, bicarbonate of soda and salt in a bowl. Lightly beat the eggs, buttermilk, maple syrup, oil and milk. Beat into the bran mixture until smooth.

3 Divide the mixture between the tins and place in a preheated oven, 200°C (400°F), Gas Mark 6, for 25 minutes, until risen and a skewer inserted into the centre comes out clean. Brush with honey and top with almonds. Serve warm.

Makes 9

PREPARATION TIME: 20 MINUTES

COOKING TIME: 25 MINUTES

OVEN TEMPERATURE: 200°C (400°F), GAS MARK 6

DOUBLE CHOC CHIP

150 g (6 oz) plain chocolate, broken into pieces

75 g (3 oz) cocoa powder

350 g (12½ oz) self-raising flour

3½ teaspoons baking powder

75 g (3 oz) dark soft brown sugar

150 g (6 oz) plain chocolate polka dots

370 ml (13 fl oz) milk

6 tablespoons (90 ml) vegetable oil

2 teaspoons (10 ml) vanilla essence

1 egg and 1 egg yolk, beaten together

1 Grease and line the bases of 9 muffin tins.

2 Melt the chocolate in a bowl over a pan of simmering water.

3 Mix together the cocoa, flour and baking powder in a bowl. Beat in the chocolate and remaining ingredients until smooth.

4 Divide the mixture between the tins, set on a baking sheet and place in a preheated oven, 200°C (425°F), Gas Mark 7, for 20 minutes, until well risen and a skewer inserted into the centre comes out clean. Serve warm.

Makes 9

PREPARATION TIME: 20 MINUTES

COOKING TIME: 20 MINUTES

OVEN TEMPERATURE: 220°C (425°F), GAS MARK 7

WHITE CHOCOLATE AND PECAN

*275 g (10 oz) white chocolate,
    broken into pieces*
450 g (1 lb) plain flour
3½ teaspoons baking powder
75 g (3 oz) caster sugar
50 g (2 oz) pecan nuts, chopped
370 ml (13 fl oz) milk
6 tablespoons (90 ml) vegetable oil
2 teaspoons (10 ml) vanilla essence
1 egg and 1 egg yolk, beaten together
2 tablespoons icing sugar, to dust

1 Grease and line the bases of 9 muffin tins.

2 Melt 150 g (6 oz) of the white chocolate in a bowl over a pan of simmering water.

3 Mix the flour and baking powder in a large bowl, and then beat in the melted chocolate and all the remaining ingredients except the icing sugar, until smooth.

4 Divide the mixture between the prepared muffin tins and place in a preheated oven, 220°C (425°F), Gas Mark 7, for 25 minutes, until risen and a skewer inserted into the centre comes out clean. Serve warm, dusted with the icing sugar.

Makes 9

PREPARATION TIME: 20 MINUTES

COOKING TIME: 25 MINUTES

OVEN TEMPERATURE: 220°C (425°F), GAS MARK 7

APPLE AND GOLDEN SYRUP

450 g (1 lb) plain flour
4 tablespoons (60 ml) golden syrup
90 g (3½ oz) light soft brown sugar
100 g (4 oz) butter, softened
75 ml (2½ fl oz) milk
2 teaspoons bicarbonate of soda
2 teaspoons ground cinnamon
½ teaspoon ground mixed spice
½ teaspoon salt
2 eggs, beaten
*675 g (1½ lb) cooking apples, peeled,
    cored and grated*
75 g (3 oz) walnuts, chopped

1 Grease and line the bases of 9 muffin tins.

2 In a large bowl, beat together all the ingredients except the apples and walnuts, until smooth, and then stir in the grated apples and chopped walnuts.

3 Divide the mixture between the prepared muffin tins, set on a baking sheet and place in a preheated oven, 190°C (375°F), Gas Mark 5, for 25 minutes, or until the muffins are well risen and a skewer inserted into the centre comes out clean. Serve warm.

Makes 9

PREPARATION TIME: 25 MINUTES

COOKING TIME: 25 MINUTES

OVEN TEMPERATURE: 190°C (375°F), GAS MARK 5

BLUEBERRY

375 g (13 oz) plain flour
200 g (7 oz) caster sugar
1½ tablespoons baking powder
½ teaspoon salt
150 g (6 oz) butter, cubed
1 egg and 1 egg yolk, beaten together
170 ml (6 fl oz) milk
grated rind of 1 lemon
1 teaspoon (5 ml) vanilla essence
150 g (6 oz) frozen blueberries

1 Grease and line the bases of 9 muffin tins.

2 Mix together the flour, sugar, baking powder and salt. Rub in the butter until the mixture resembles breadcrumbs. Beat together the egg and egg yolk, milk, lemon rind and vanilla essence. Stir into the flour mixture with the blueberries.

3 Divide between the tins, set on a baking sheet and place in a preheated oven, 200°C (400°F), Gas Mark 6, for 30 minutes, until risen and a skewer inserted into the centre comes out clean. Serve warm.

Makes 9

PREPARATION TIME: 25 MINUTES

COOKING TIME: 30 MINUTES

OVEN TEMPERATURE: 200°C (400°F), GAS MARK 6

Novelty Cakes

MAN'S BEST FRIEND

400 g (14 oz) soft margarine

275 g (10 oz) caster sugar

275 g (10 oz) self-raising flour, sifted

5 eggs, beaten

225 g (8 oz) icing sugar, sifted

4 drops of vanilla essence

900 g (2 lb) ready-to-roll fondant icing

green, blue, black, brown, red and
orange food colouring

You will also need

568 ml (1 pint) and 1.1 litre (2 pint)
pudding basins

20 cm (8 inch) square silver cake board

15 cm (6 inches) narrow red tartan ribbon

Spread a little buttercream over the larger cake, put the smaller cake on top and trim to form the head.

1 Grease both pudding basins and line the bases with greased grease-proof paper. Beat together 275 g (10 oz) of the margarine, the caster sugar, flour and eggs, until smooth. Spoon two-thirds of the mixture into the large basin and the remainder into the small basin. Make a well in the centre of each.

2 Place the large basin in a pre-heated oven, 160°C (325°F), Gas Mark 3, for 45-50 minutes, and the small basin for 40 minutes, or until a skewer inserted into the centre comes out clean. Leave the cakes in

Shape all the features, and the bone and flowers, and attach to the cake as shown.

the basins to cool for 15 minutes, then turn out on to a wire rack and leave to cool completely.

3 To make the buttercream: cream together the remaining margarine, the icing sugar and the vanilla essence.

4 To decorate the cake: colour 225 g (8 oz) of the fondant green. Roll it out thinly and cut into 5 mm (¼ inch) strips. Alternatively, feed the fondant through a pasta machine on the spaghetti setting. Put the icing on the dampened cake board to give a grass effect.

5 Level the tops of the cakes and put the large cake on the board. Spread a little buttercream over the top of the cake and put the small cake on top; trim the base of the small cake to form the dog's head. Spread the remaining buttercream over both cakes.

6 Shape the paws, muzzle and ears from 125 g (5 oz) of the white (uncoloured) fondant. Colour 3 pieces of fondant, each 15 g (½ oz),

MAN'S BEST FRIEND

blue, black and brown; colour 25 g (1 oz) red and a little orange. Use the blue and black to make the eyes and nose, brown for the bone, red and orange for the tongue and the flowers. Fix them all in place with a little water.

7 Roll out the remaining white fondant thinly and cut into 5 mm (¼ inch) strips or feed through a pasta machine on the spaghetti setting. Press the strips all over the body, trimming into shape around the head and nose. Tie a bow in the ribbon and fix it to the head, pulling a few strands of fondant hair over it.

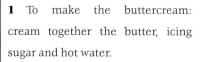

Arrange the fondant 'hair' all over the dog, leaving just its eyes, nose and paws uncovered, pressing the fondant gently but firmly into the buttercream.

SAY IT WITH FLOWERS

50 g (2 oz) butter, softened
100 g (4 oz) icing sugar, sifted
½ tablespoon (7.5 ml) hot water
15 cm (6 inch) square sponge cake
6 tablespoons lemon curd
1.1 kg (2½ lb) ready-to-roll fondant
  icing
¼ teaspoon gum tragacanth
yellow, orange, green and red
  food colouring

YOU WILL ALSO NEED
25 x 20 cm (10 x 8 inch) silver
  cake board
5-petalled flower cutter
small paintbrush

1 To make the buttercream: cream together the butter, icing sugar and hot water.

2 Trim the top of the cake level if necessary, split the cake in half horizontally and sandwich together with lemon curd. Make 3 marks at equal distances apart along the bottom edge of the cake. Using a sharp knife and beginning at the top left corner, cut a diagonal line through the cake to the nearest mark to give a triangular wedge. Repeat on other side. Arrange as shown, top right.

3 Put the cake on the board. Cover completely with buttercream. Roll out 400 g (14 oz) of the fondant and use it to cover the top and sides of the cake. Trim the edges and reserve the trimmings.

To create this unusually shaped cake, simply trim the sides of a 15 cm (6 inch) square sponge cake and re-arrange as shown.

Working quickly, because gum tragacanth will make the fondant harden, cut out the narcissi and pinch the back of each of the 5 petals into shape.

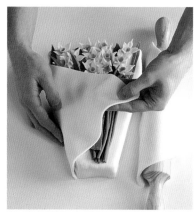

Wrap the bunch of flowers in 2 triangles of white fondant, which are fixed to the sides of the cake with a little water.

4 Knead the trimmings together with another 150 g (6 oz) of the fondant and the gum tragacanth — once you have added the gum tragacanth the fondant hardens quickly. Roll 15 g (½ oz) into a 5 x 4 cm (2 x 1½ inch) rectangle for the card and leave to dry. Colour 125 g (5 oz) of the fondant and gum tragacanth mixture yellow and the remainder orange. Roll out the yellow fondant and, using the flower cutter, cut out 12 flowers. Lightly pinch the petals together and leave to dry overnight on crumpled foil. Divide the orange fondant into 12 and roll each into a ball. Insert a cocktail stick into each ball and gently roll on a surface to make cup shapes for the centres of the narcissi, as shown, left. Leave to dry.

5 Colour 225 g (8 oz) of the fondant green. Divide 100 g (4 oz) into 12 and roll into lengths for the flower stems. Roll out the remaining 100 g (4 oz) and cut out 9 long, flat leaves. Mark a vein down the centre of each leaf. Fix the leaves and stems to the cake with water.

6 Fix the centres to the narcissi with a little water, then arrange the flowers on the cake and fix in place with a little water.

7 Divide the remaining 325 g (12 oz) of white fondant into 2 equal pieces. Roll out 1 piece into an equilateral triangle with 20 cm (8 inch) sides. Fix to the side of cake with a little water and wrap over the stems to the opposite side of the cake, then trim. Repeat with the remaining fondant on the other side to make a wrapping paper effect.

8 Paint red dots on the wrapping paper and a message on the card. Fix the card to the cake with water.

FISHY TALE

Smooth the 'watery' blue fondant over the top of the cake, then down the sides and over the cake board.

Each of the small pieces is quite straightforward to make, as shown.

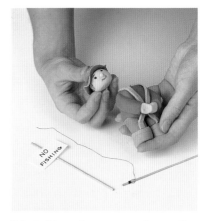

Make the fisherman in separate parts, then assemble, fixing with a little water.

100 g (4 oz) butter, softened

225 g (8 oz) icing sugar, sifted

¼ teaspoon vanilla essence

1 tablespoon (15 ml) hot water

20 cm (8 inch) round sponge cake

blue, black, green, yellow, orange, red,
*   brown and pink food colouring*

1 kg (2¼ lb) ready-to-roll
*   fondant icing*

¼ teaspoon gum tragacanth

YOU WILL ALSO NEED

30 cm (12 inch) round gold cake board

8 large cake-decorating flower stamens

2 bamboo skewers

15 cm (6 inches) black cotton

fine paintbrush

1 To make the buttercream: cream together the butter, all but 2 tablespoons of the icing sugar, the vanilla essence and water until the mixture is light and fluffy.

2 Slice the cake in half horizontally and sandwich together with half the buttercream. Reserve 2 tablespoons of the buttercream and spread the rest over the top and sides of the cake. Put the cake on the cake board, then dampen the board edges with water.

3 Roughly knead a little blue food colouring into 550 g (1¼ lb) of the fondant – it should not be blended to give an even colour. Roll out the fondant on a surface lightly dusted with icing sugar and use to cover the cake and board. Trim off any excess fondant.

4 Knead the gum tragacanth into the remaining fondant. Colour 75 g (3 oz) grey, 125 g (5 oz) green, 50 g (2 oz) yellow, 25 g (1 oz) orange and 75 g (3 oz) red. Shape the pebbles, leaves, 3 ducks and 2 fish and reserve the trimmings. Use a tiny amount of white (uncoloured) fondant to make the eyes; paint the centres with black food colouring. Roll out 25 g (1 oz) of white fondant

and cut out 7 water lilies. Roll 7 balls out of the red fondant for the centre of the flowers. Paint the stamens brown. Shape the fisherman from the remaining green, red and grey fondant. Colour 25 g (1 oz) of the fondant pink and use to shape the hands and head. Paint on the features and fix together with water. Leave all the shapes to dry overnight.

5 Fix all the pieces on to the cake using the reserved buttercream. Write the message on a piece of paper, fix it to one of the skewers and push it into the cake. Tie the cotton on to the other skewer and fix it in the man's hand. Fix the cotton into the fish's mouth with a little water. Mix the reserved icing sugar with a little water and drizzle it around the fisherman and fish.

Penguin

275 g (10 oz) soft margarine

275 g (10 oz) caster sugar

275 g (10 oz) self-raising flour, sifted

5 eggs, beaten

275 g (10 oz) butter, softened

550 g (1¼ lb) icing sugar, sifted

¼ teaspoon vanilla essence

1 tablespoon (15 ml) hot water

450 g (1 lb) ready-to-roll fondant icing

black and orange food colouring

You will also need

568 ml (1 pint) and 1.1 litre (2 pint)
  pudding basins

20 cm (8 inch) round silver cake board

piping gun or bag set

small star nozzle

fine paintbrush

1 Grease both pudding basins and line the bases with greased greaseproof paper. Beat together the margarine, caster sugar, flour and eggs until smooth. Spoon two-thirds of the mixture into the large basin and the remainder into the small basin. Make a well in the centre of each.

2 Place the large basin in a preheated oven, 160°C (325°F), Gas Mark 3, for 50-55 minutes, and the small basin for 40 minutes, or until a skewer inserted into the centres comes out clean. Leave the cakes in the basins for 15 minutes, then turn out and cool on a wire rack.

3 To make the buttercream: cream together the butter, icing sugar, vanilla essence and water.

4 Dampen the cake board. Roll out half the fondant and cover the cake board. Slice the cakes in half horizontally and sandwich them together with a little buttercream.

5 Cut a thick slice from the front of the large cake and then cut it in half to make 2 wedges. Spread a little buttercream over the top of the large cake and put the small cake on top. Place the cake on the board. Spread buttercream on the inside of the wedges and fix them on either side of the cake to form wings, as shown below.

6 Thinly roll out half of the remaining fondant and cut out a large semicircle. Fix the fondant semicircle to the front of the cake with buttercream.

7 Colour the remaining buttercream black and spoon it into a piping gun or bag fitted with a small star nozzle. Pipe buttercream stars, for feathers, all over both cakes so they are completely covered.

8 Colour 50 g (2 oz) of the fondant orange and shape the beak and feet, as shown below. Stamp out 2 white fondant rounds and paint on the eyes and nostrils, using black food colouring. Press the eyes and beak into the black buttercream and stand the feet on the board. Cut the remaining white fondant into cubes to make blocks of ice and arrange them on the board.

Cut a thick slice from the front of the large cake and then cut it in half to make 'wings'.

To create black buttercream, you will need to use a whole 22 g (1 oz) pot of black paste food colouring.

The beak and feet are made from 50 g (2 oz) of orange fondant.

BUNNY IN A BARROW

Roll 100 g (4 oz) dark brown fondant into 2 long and 2 short log shapes and mark a woodgrain effect with a cocktail stick.

The rabbit is made from 450 g (1 lb) of pale yellow fondant; make the body, head, ears and paws separately, then assemble on the cake.

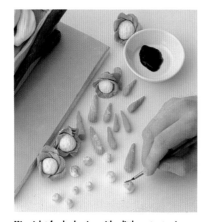

Mix violet food colouring with a little water to give a less intense colour, then paint the balls of white fondant to resemble turnips.

100 g (4 oz) butter, softened
225 g (8 oz) icing sugar, sifted
few drops of vanilla essence
1 teaspoon (5 ml) hot water
15 cm (6 inch) square sponge cake
4 tablespoons apricot jam
1.6 kg (3 lb 9 oz) ready-to-roll
    fondant icing
green, brown, yellow, violet, orange,
    red and black food colouring

YOU WILL ALSO NEED

25 cm (10 inch) square cake board
ruler
cocktail stick
fine paintbrush

1 To make the buttercream: cream together the butter, icing sugar, vanilla essence and water until smooth and fluffy.

2 Trim the sides of the cake to form a rectangle. Slice the cake in half horizontally and sandwich together with a third of the buttercream and all the apricot jam. Spread the remaining buttercream over the top and sides of the cake.

3 Colour 400 g (14 oz) of the fondant green. Dampen the cake board. Roll out 325 g (12 oz) of the green fondant on a surface lightly dusted with icing sugar and use it to cover the board. Trim the edges.

4 Colour 275 g (10 oz) of the fondant light brown and cover the top and sides of the cake. Using a ruler, make indented lines around the sides of the cake to look like planks of wood. Colour 150 g (6 oz) of the fondant dark brown and use 100 g (4 oz) of it to make the handles for the barrow. Mark the woodgrain effect with a cocktail stick, as shown, left. Fix the handles to the cake with a little water. Use the remaining dark brown fondant to make a wheel, and fix in place.

5 Colour 450 g (1 lb) of the fondant pale yellow and make the rabbit, as shown. Use 25 g (1 oz) of white fondant to make the details on the face, ears and paws. Mark the claws with a sharp knife. Colour 50 g (2 oz) of the fondant violet and make the hat. Fix the rabbit and hat to the cake with a little water.

6 Colour 75 g (3 oz) of the fondant orange and shape into carrots. Mark the details with a knife. Divide 75 g (3 oz) of the white fondant into 5

balls and roll on the coarse side of a grater to give a texture to these 'cauliflower heads'. Use half of the remaining green fondant to make cauliflower leaves. Divide 50 g (2 oz) of white fondant into 12 little balls. Paint the tops of each with a little watered-down violet food colouring, to resemble turnips.

7 Fix the vegetables around the bunny with a little water. Use watered-down red food colouring to paint the nose and black colouring for the details on the face. Push the remaining green fondant through a sieve to make tufts of grass. Fix to the board with a little water.

CLOWN

550 g (1¼ lb) soft margarine

325 g (12 oz) caster sugar

325 g (12 oz) self-raising flour

6 eggs, beaten

225 g (8 oz) icing sugar

1 tablespoon (15 ml) hot water

2 jam Swiss rolls

850 g (1 lb 14 oz) ready-to-roll
   fondant icing

blue, pink, yellow, black, red and
   orange food colouring

YOU WILL ALSO NEED

568 ml (1 pint) and 1.1 litre (2 pint)
   pudding basins

25 cm (10 inch) square silver cake board

blue card

3 small Christmas tree baubles

1 Grease both pudding basins and line the bases with greased greaseproof paper. Beat together 325 g (12 oz) of the margarine with the caster sugar, flour and eggs, until smooth. Spoon two-thirds of the mixture into the large basin and the remainder into the small basin. Make a well in the centre of each.

2 Place in a preheated oven, 160°C (325°F), Gas Mark 3, for 45 minutes, or until a skewer inserted into the centre of the cakes comes out clean. Turn out the cakes and cool on a wire rack.

3 To make the buttercream: cream together the remaining margarine, icing sugar and hot water.

Use 2 Swiss rolls, halved lengthways, to make the arms and legs.

4 Using a long sharp knife, level the tops of the cakes. Trim to shape the head and body. Sandwich with buttercream and place on the cake board, as shown above. Cut the Swiss rolls in half lengthways and fix to the cake with half the buttercream to make the legs and arms. Reserve 1 tablespoon of buttercream and spread the remainder over the cakes.

5 Thinly roll out 150 g (6 oz) of the fondant to a 30 cm (12 inch) circle to cover the head. Shape the hands from 50 g (2 oz) of the fondant.

6 Colour 75 g (3 oz) of the fondant blue to cover the legs and make the patches. Colour 225 g (8 oz) of the fondant pink, roll out and use to make the jacket.

7 Colour 100 g (4 oz) of the fondant yellow and use to make the bow, buttons and cuffs. Colour 75 g (3 oz) of fondant black for the shoes and eyes; and 25 g (1 oz) red to

Cut the jacket in separate parts and then arrange on the cake, overlapping slightly.

make the nose and mouth. Use the yellow trimmings for the smile.

8 Fix the hands, buttons, bow, cuffs, patches and face with water. Paint a check pattern on the trousers with black food colouring. Use the reserved buttercream to fix the shoes to the legs. Colour the remaining fondant icing orange and use to make the hair; fix to the head with water.

9 Cut a 25 cm (10 inch) circle from card. Cut away a quarter, then glue to form a cone. Glue on the baubles and place on the head.

Colour about 75 g (3 oz) of fondant orange, cut into strips and fix to the head with a little water.

MR FIXIT

100 g (4 oz) butter

325 g (12 oz) icing sugar, sifted

few drops of vanilla essence

1 teaspoon (5 ml) hot water

15 cm (6 inch) square sponge cake

1.1 kg (2½ lb) ready-to-roll
*   fondant icing*

blue, black, green, brown, pink and
*   yellow food colouring*

¼ teaspoon gum tragacanth

silver food paint

YOU WILL ALSO NEED

25 cm (10 inch) square silver cake board

fine paintbrush

1   To make the buttercream: cream together the butter, 225 g (8 oz) of the icing sugar, the vanilla essence and water.

2   Cut the cake in half vertically and trim the edges to soften them. Using the tip of a knife, mark a rectangle on top of one half, leaving a 2.5 cm (1 inch) border around the edge. Cut out to a depth of 1 cm (½ inch). Spread buttercream over both halves.

3   Roll out 450 g (1 lb) of the fondant on a surface dusted with icing sugar and use it to cover each half cake. Using a little buttercream, sandwich the halves together to make the sink unit.

4   Dampen the cake board. Roll out 325 g (12 oz) of the fondant and cover the cake board. Using the back of a knife, mark squares diagonally across the fondant on the board. Trim the edges and position the sink on the board.

5   In a small bowl, mix the remaining icing sugar with 3 tablespoons (45 ml) cold water and a little blue food colouring. Pour into the sink until level with the top edge. Cover the remaining blue icing with clingfilm and reserve.

6   Mix a little water with some black food colouring and paint every second square on the board to create a tiled effect.

7   Knead the gum tragacanth into the remaining fondant and use a little to make the taps, tools and door. Leave to dry. Divide the remaining fondant into several pieces and colour appropriately, as shown, below right, then use to shape the plumber's body and bag.

8   Put some of the tools in the bag and the remainder on the cake board. Paint the tools and taps silver. Fix the door to the sink with water. Paint behind the door black and paint the details on the cupboard using yellow food colouring. Use the reserved blue icing to pour over the edge of the sink and make puddles on the board.

Cut the sponge cake in half, then mark a rim on one half and hollow out a little of the cake to form a shallow sink.

Carefully pour blue icing into the fondant-covered sink until it is level with the top edge. Cover the remaining icing with clingfilm until needed.

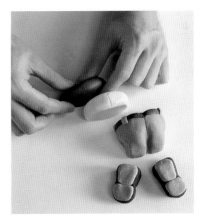

The plumber's rear end is assembled from various pieces of coloured fondant; it has been mixed with gum tragacanth so it will set rock hard.

HAPPY CAMPING

150 g (6 oz) soft margarine

150 g (6 oz) caster sugar

150 g (6 oz) self-raising flour

3 eggs, beaten

4 drops of vanilla essence

1½ tablespoons (22.5 ml) milk

100 g (4 oz) butter

225 g (8 oz) icing sugar

750 g (1 lb 11 oz) ready-to-roll
    fondant icing

black, orange, pink, blue, brown, red,
    yellow and green food colouring

25 g (1 oz) desiccated coconut

YOU WILL ALSO NEED

25 cm (10 inch) square silver cake
    board

coloured twine

cocktail stick

1 Grease and line a 900 g (2 lb) loaf tin. Beat together the margarine, caster sugar, flour, eggs, 2 drops of vanilla essence and milk until smooth. Spoon into the tin and make a well in the centre. Place in a preheated oven, 160°C (325°F), Gas Mark 3, for 40 minutes, or until a skewer inserted into the centre comes out clean. Turn out and cool on a wire rack.

2 To make the buttercream: cream together the butter, icing sugar and remaining 2 drops of vanilla essence.

3 Using a sharp knife, level the top of the cake and cut off the ends. Cut the cake in half diagonally lengthways. Sandwich with a quarter of the buttercream to form a long pyramid. Spread buttercream all over the cake.

4 Colour 100 g (4 oz) of the fondant black. Roll out half and use to cover one end of the cake.

5 Colour 450 g (1 lb) of the fondant orange; reserve 25 g (1 oz) and cut off a quarter of the remainder; roll it out and cut out 2 triangles to cover the ends of the cake. Roll out the remaining orange fondant and use to cover the rest of the cake. Mark the 'seams' and 'zip' with a cocktail stick

6 Put the cake on the board. Cut the orange fondant at the

Cut the loaf-shaped cake in half diagonally lengthways and turn the 2 halves back to back.

Make all the small pieces separately, as shown, then assemble, fixing with a little water.

black end of the cake and peel back the tent flap.

7 Colour 50 g (2 oz) of the fondant pink and shape the head and hands. Colour 25 g (1 oz) of the fondant blue and shape the arms. Use half the remaining black fondant for the hair and eyes. Fix in place with water.

8 Colour 75 g (3 oz) of the fondant brown and use to shape the wood, rucksack, frying pan and pegs.

Colour 15 g (½ oz) of fondant red for the flames. Shape the sleeping bag using half of the reserved orange fondant. Shape the blackbird using the remaining orange and black fondant. Shape the egg and paint the yolk yellow. Fix all the shapes in place with a little water.

9 Colour the coconut with green food colouring. Sprinkle freely around the cake. Fix the twine and pegs in position with water.

BOXING RING

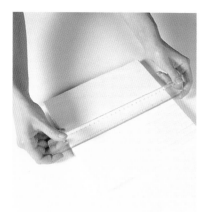

Using the side of a ruler, mark regularly spaced lines in the fondant on the cake board to look like planks of wood.

Dilute the brown food colouring with a little water and brush over the 'planks'; for a realistic wood effect avoid making the colour too even.

To make the figures, first make an oval shape and make cuts for the arms and legs (above right), then model the arms and legs in more detail (above left).

75 g (3 oz) butter, softened

150 g (6 oz) icing sugar, sifted

2 teaspoons (10 ml) hot water

15 cm (6 inch) square sponge cake

2 tablespoons apricot jam

675 g (1½ lb) ready-to-roll
   fondant icing

brown, pink, blue, red, black, green
   food colouring

YOU WILL ALSO NEED

10 inch (25 cm) square silver cake
   board

1 bamboo skewer

125 cm (50 inches) narrow ribbon

1 To make the buttercream: cream together the butter, icing sugar and water until smooth. Slice the cake in half horizontally and sandwich together with buttercream and apricot jam.

2 Dampen the cake board. Roll out 100 g (4 oz) of the fondant and cover the board. Trim the edges. Using the side of a ruler, mark lines in the fondant 1 cm (½ inch) apart. Mark the planks, woodgrain and nails with a cocktail stick.

3 Roll out 325 g (12 oz) of the fondant and cover the cake. Put the cake on the board. Mark the planks around the ring with a ruler and cocktail stick. Cut the bamboo skewer into 4, push 1 piece into each corner of the ring and secure with fondant. Cut the ribbon in half

and tie around the corner posts. Thin the brown food colouring with a little water and brush over the planks. Leave to dry.

4 Colour 100 g (4 oz) of the fondant pink and make 2 figures and the ref's head and hands. Use 20 g (¾ oz) of fondant to make the ref's shirt. Colour 15 g (½ oz) of fondant blue and 15 g (½ oz) red and use to make the shorts and the ref's shoes. Colour 25 g (1 oz) of the fondant black and shape the boots, gloves and ref's trousers. Fix to the figures with water.

5 Colour 25 g (1 oz) of the fondant green and roll out to make 2 towels. Fix one on the cake board and the other on a corner post. Roll out 25 g (1 oz) of fondant into a 20 x 4 cm (8 x 1½ inch) strip and cut into 8 rectangles for the posters. Fix the figures in the boxing ring with water.

6 Using black food colouring, paint on the hair and faces. Paint the details on the posters with red food colouring. Leave to dry.

HALLOWEEN

50 g (2 oz) butter, softened

100 g (4 oz) icing sugar, sifted

2 teaspoons (10 ml) hot water

20 cm (8 inch) round sponge cake

3 tablespoons apricot jam

325 g (12 oz) almond paste

725 g (1 lb 10 oz) ready-to-roll
    fondant icing

yellow, dark blue and black
    food colouring

6 silver balls

YOU WILL ALSO NEED

23 cm (9 inch) round cake board

fine paintbrush

1 To make the buttercream: cream together the butter, icing sugar and water until smooth and fluffy. Slice the cake in half horizontally and sandwich together with the buttercream.

2 Put the cake on the cake board. Melt the apricot jam with 1 tablespoon (15 ml) water. Brush it over the top and sides of the cake. Roll out the almond paste on a surface lightly dusted with icing sugar and use to cover the cake.

3 To decorate the cake: using a 20 cm (8 inch) round cake tin as a template, draw a circle on greaseproof paper. Draw a cloud, witch, moon and bat inside the circle. Colour 450 g (1 lb) of the fondant bright yellow, 150 g (6 oz) dark blue and 100 g (4 oz) black, leaving a tiny

piece white. Brush the sides of the cake with a little water. Roll out the yellow fondant and use it to cover the cake and board. Trim off the excess and reserve the trimmings.

4 Fix the drawing on top of the cake with pins and prick through the paper on the inside edge of the pencil lines with a pin. Prick out all the shapes except the moon and then remove the paper.

5 Using a small, pointed knife, cut the fondant along the pin marks and carefully remove each shape to use as templates. Roll out 100 g (4 oz) of the blue fondant, just larger than the cloud template. Put the cut-out yellow cloud on top of the blue fondant and cut around it. Peel away the blue and reserve the yellow. Fit the blue cloud into place on the cake, overlapping the edge.

6 Roll out the black fondant and cut out the witch and bat shapes using the yellow templates. Fit into place. Pin the drawing back on the top of the cake and mark out the moon with a pin. Cut out and replace the shape with rolled-out yellow trimmings. Push silver balls into the blue fondant for stars. Use tiny white and black fondant trimmings for the eye of the moon.

7 Roll out the remaining blue and yellow fondant into 30 cm (12 inch) lengths. Twist together and fix around the cake with a little water.

Pin your paper design on to the fondant-covered cake, then prick around the designs with a pin. Following the pinpricks, cut out the designs from the fondant.

Use the fondant cut from the top of the cake as templates to cut out the fondant design, slightly larger than the templates.

Fit the fondant shapes into the spaces left on top of the cake, pushing them gently into place and smoothing the fondant.

ON THE ROAD

100 g (4 oz) butter, softened

225 g (8 oz) icing sugar, sifted

1 teaspoon vanilla essence

800 g (1¾ lb) ready-to-roll
    fondant icing

blue, black, purple, green, orange,
    yellow and red food colouring

15 cm (6 inch) square sponge cake

black piping icing gel

YOU WILL ALSO NEED

20 cm (8 inch) square cake board

1 To make the buttercream: cream together the butter, icing sugar and vanilla essence until smooth.

2 Colour 100 g (4 oz) of the fondant sky blue and 50 g (2 oz) grey. Roll out and lift on to the dampened cake board. Colour 225 g (8 oz) of the fondant in a selection of colours for the rainbow, grass and birds. Roll out on a surface lightly dusted with icing sugar and cut out the rainbow strips, grass and birds. Roll out 50 g (2 oz) of white fondant and cut out the clouds. Dampen the fondant and lay on the board, fitting the pieces together to make the background.

3 Cut out a car shape from the cake, discarding the trimmings. Slice the cake in half horizontally and sandwich together with half the buttercream. Spread the remaining buttercream over the top and sides of the cake.

4 Colour 275 g (10 oz) of the fondant bright blue and use to cover the cake, trimming around the base. Carefully lift the covered cake on to the board, positioning it on the road.

5 Thinly roll out the remaining white fondant and cut out the car windows. Colour 25 g (1 oz) of the fondant yellow and 25 g (1 oz) black. Stamp out rounds, one smaller than the other, for the wheels. Fix in place with water.

6 Use the remaining yellow fondant trimmings for the bumpers, and red and white trimmings for headlights. Fix to the cake with water. Pipe the doors and handles with the black piping icing gel.

Cut out a car shape from the sponge cake, discarding the trimmings.

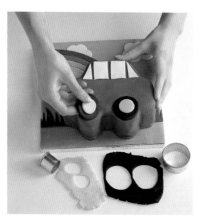

Cover the cake with buttercream and bright blue fondant; fix the windows and wheels with water.

SNOWMAN

250 g (9 oz) butter

250 g (9 oz) caster sugar

5 eggs, beaten

150 g (6 oz) plain flour

240 g (8½ oz) self-raising flour

grated rind and juice of 1 orange

FOR THE BUTTERCREAM

150 g (6 oz) granulated sugar

4 egg yolks

325 g (12 oz) butter, cut in pieces

100 g (4 oz) white chocolate

TO DECORATE

900 g (2 lb) ready-to-roll fondant icing

blue, black, brown, green, yellow and
    red food colouring

cornflour, to dust

225 g (8 oz) almond paste

225 g (8 oz) icing sugar

YOU WILL ALSO NEED

568 ml (1 pint) and 1.1 litre (2 pint)
    pudding basins

6 sheets kitchen paper

25 cm (10 inch) round silver cake
    board

3 x 15 cm (6 inch) wooden skewers

6 cocktail sticks

holly leaf cutter

SNOWMAN

Slice the 2 cakes horizontally into 3 layers. Spread each of the layers with some of the white chocolate buttercream and sandwich together.

Push 3 wooden skewers halfway into the larger cake and push the smaller cake down on to them. When you come to cut the cake, don't forget the skewers.

Shape the arms and feet from almond paste and attach to the cake with cocktail sticks – 2 for each arm and 1 for each foot.

1 Grease the base and sides of the pudding basins. Beat together the butter and caster sugar until light and fluffy. Gradually stir in the beaten eggs. Sift the flours together and fold them into the mixture. Fold in the orange rind, together with 2 tablespoons (30 ml) of the juice. Spoon two-thirds of the mixture into the large basin and the remainder into the small basin.

2 Place in a preheated oven, 160°C (325°F), Gas Mark 3, for 1¾ hours for the large basin and 1½ hours for the small basin, or until a skewer inserted into the centre of the cakes comes out clean. Turn out and leave to cool on a wire rack.

3 To make the buttercream: put the granulated sugar into a heavy-bottomed saucepan with 6 tablespoons (90 ml) water and heat gently, stirring occasionally, until the sugar dissolves. Bring to the boil and boil steadily for about 5 minutes, without stirring, until the temperature reaches 110°C (225°F) on a sugar thermometer, or until a small amount dropped into a bowl of ice-cold water forms a soft ball. Whisk the egg yolks in a large bowl until they are pale and thick. Gradually whisk in the hot syrup and continue whisking until the mixture is cool and thick. Then gradually whisk in the butter until smooth. Melt the white chocolate in a bowl set over a pan of simmering water and then whisk it into the egg mixture. Chill.

4 To decorate the cake: colour 225 g (8 oz) of the fondant dark blue and roll it out to a circle about 5 mm (¼ inch) thick. Scrunch some kitchen paper into a dome and mould the fondant over it to form a hat. Pinch the brim to flute. Roll 50 g (2 oz) of the white fondant into snowballs. Leave to dry.

5 Slice both the cooled cakes horizontally into 3 equal layers. Using a palette knife, sandwich the layers of each cake together with a quarter of the white chocolate buttercream. Cut a thin slice from the top of both cakes to level the surface. Holding the cake layers in place, trim away the sides of each of the cakes to form a rounder shape.

6 On a surface lightly dusted with cornflour, roll out 250 g (8 oz) of the white fondant and use to cover the cake board. Use a little of the buttercream to fix the large cake (the body of the snowman) to the board. Push 3 skewers halfway into the body and push the smaller cake down on to them.

7 Take 2 pieces of almond paste, each 75 g (3 oz), and roll them into 7 cm (3 inch) sausage shapes for the arms. Halve the remaining almond paste and roll into 2 balls for the feet. Use 2 cocktail sticks to fix each

Spread the buttercream over the cake, making sure the sponge is completely covered, then smooth the buttercream and chill for 2 hours.

Sift the icing sugar over the snowman, using a small knife to pat icing sugar on to any areas which remain uncovered, and into any crevices.

Use the brown, red, green and yellow fondant to make the robin, the snowman's nose and the holly berries and leaves.

arm to the body, and 1 cocktail stick to position each foot.

8 Lightly beat the buttercream to return it to a spreading consistency. Spread the buttercream all over the cake, smoothing it with a palette knife. Chill in the refrigerator for 2 hours, until the buttercream becomes firm.

9 Spoon all but 1 tablespoon of the icing sugar into a sieve and dredge the snowman. Using a small knife, pat the icing sugar on to any uncovered areas.

10 Colour 75 g (3 oz) of the fondant black and use some of it to make 6 small circles. Reserve 2 for the eyes and make 4 buttons, marking the thread holes on the buttons with a cocktail stick. With the remaining black icing, shape a small pipe and roll 6 small balls for the mouth.

11 Colour 25 g (1 oz) of the fondant brown, 50 g (2 oz) green, a little yellow, and the rest red. Model the robin with the brown, yellow and a little of the red fondant. Use some of the red fondant to form the nose and to roll a few holly berries. Roll out the green fondant and cut out the holly leaves.

12 Roll out the remaining red fondant to make a scarf measuring 48 x 4 cm (19 x 1½ inches). Fringe the ends of the scarf and wrap it around the snowman's neck. Press the features on to the face. Pop the pipe in

Shape the black fondant into 6 circles for the snowman's eyes and buttons, 6 small balls for the mouth, and a small pipe.

To finish the cake, press all the fondant features into the buttercream, add the hat and scarf, and fix the robin and holly with a little water.

the mouth and press the buttons on to the front of the body. Fix on the robin, the hat, the holly and the berries. Dredge the reserved icing sugar over the hat.

Chocolate Dreams

SHEER INDULGENCE

225 g (8 oz) soft margarine

350 g (12½ oz) caster sugar

4 eggs, plus 3 yolks

150 g (6 oz) self-raising flour, sifted

50 g (2 oz) orange-flavoured plain
   chocolate, melted

75 g (3 oz) cocoa powder

4 tablespoons (60 ml) liquid glucose

225g (8 oz) plain chocolate, melted

250 g (9 oz) butter, softened

1 Grease and line an 18 cm (7 inch) square cake tin.

2 Put the margarine, 225 g (8 oz) of the sugar, 4 eggs and the flour into a large bowl. Using an electric whisk, beat for 3-4 minutes, until smooth, then beat in 1 tablespoon (15 ml) hot water. Stir in the orange-flavoured chocolate and 50 g (2 oz) of the cocoa. Spoon into the tin; make a dip in the centre.

3 Place in a preheated oven, 160°C (325°F), Gas Mark 3, for 1 hour or until risen. Leave to cool in the tin for 10 minutes, then turn out and cool on a wire rack.

4 Meanwhile, stir the liquid glucose into the melted plain chocolate. Continue stirring until the mixture leaves the sides of the bowl clean. Put into a plastic bag and chill until firm but not hard.

5 Dissolve the remaining sugar with 5 tablespoons (75 ml) water in a heavy-bottomed saucepan over a low heat. Bring to the boil and boil until the temperature reaches 110°C (225°F) on a sugar thermometer, or until a drop of syrup forms a thread when pulled between your thumb and forefinger (drop it on to a saucer first).

6 Put the 3 egg yolks into a bowl. Whisking continuously, slowly pour in the hot syrup in a steady stream. Continue whisking until the mixture is cold.

7 Mix the remaining cocoa with 2 tablespoons (30 ml) hot water. Beat in the butter, adding a little at a time, until thick and glossy. Slice the cake in half horizontally, then sandwich together with one-third

of the chocolate buttercream. Using a palette knife, spread the remaining chocolate buttercream over the top and sides of the cake.

8 Divide the chocolate and glucose mixture into 4 equal pieces. Knead 1 piece until soft and roll out to a 50 x 9 cm (20 x 3½ inch) rectangle; reserve the trimmings.

9 Crimp the rectangle roughly and drape it around 1 side of the cake. Repeat the process of kneading and rolling the chocolate into rectangles to cover the remaining 3 sides of the cake. Pinch the edges together at the corners.

10 Mould the trimmings into chocolate leaves, 1 rose and 2 rosebuds (see page 26) and arrange in a corner of the cake. Leave to set before serving.

Serves 16

PREPARATION TIME: 45 MINUTES, PLUS
COOLING AND CHILLING TIME

COOKING TIME: 1 HOUR

OVEN TEMPERATURE: 160°C (325°F),
GAS MARK 3

BLACK FOREST GÂTEAU

150 g (6 oz) soft margarine

150 g (6 oz) caster sugar

100 g (4 oz) self-raising flour, sifted

50 g (2 oz) cocoa powder, sifted

3 eggs, beaten

1 tablespoon (15 ml) milk

6 tablespoons (90 ml) Kirsch

4 tablespoons (60 ml) orange juice

568 ml (1 pint) double cream

397 g (14 oz) can black cherry
*   pie filling*

225 g (8 oz) plain chocolate

50 g (2 oz) white chocolate

selection of fresh leaves (e.g. rose,
*   chrysanthemum, weeping fig),*
*   wiped and dried*

icing sugar, to dust

1 Grease and line an 18 cm (7 inch) round, deep, loose-bottomed cake tin.

2 In a bowl, beat together the margarine, sugar, flour, cocoa, eggs and milk until smooth. Pour into the tin and place in a preheated oven, 160°C (325°F), Gas Mark 3, for 50 minutes or until a skewer inserted into the centre comes out clean. Turn out and cool on a wire rack. When cold, slice the cake horizontally into 3 layers, using a long, serrated knife.

3 Mix the Kirsch with the orange juice and drizzle a little over each layer. Whip the cream until soft peaks form. Put 1 layer of cake on to a serving plate and spread with

one-third of the cream. Spoon over half of the cherry pie filling. Using a fish slice, lift the second cake layer on top, spread with half of the remaining cream and the remaining cherry pie filling. Put the third cake layer on top.

4 Spread the top and sides of the cake with the remaining cream. Put in the refrigerator while making the chocolate curls.

5 Melt 150 g (6 oz) of the plain chocolate in a bowl set over a pan of simmering water. Spread the chocolate in a thin layer over a marble slab or a cold metal baking sheet. Chill for 5 minutes, until the chocolate has set hard.

6 Using a flexible metal palette knife, press down on to the chocolate and pull across to form curls.

7 Using a pair of tweezers, carefully position the chocolate curls around the sides of the cake. Return any excess set chocolate to the bowl, place over a pan of simmering water and melt together with the remaining 50 g (2 oz) of plain chocolate. Melt the white chocolate in a separate bowl.

8 Dip a brush in the melted chocolate. Hold 1 of the leaves by the stem and carefully brush the back with either dark or white chocolate, making sure that the chocolate does not run over the edge. Leave on a wire rack for 15

minutes or until set. Repeat with the remaining leaves.

9 Starting at the pointed end of the leaf, carefully peel away the

leaves from the chocolate and arrange the chocolate leaves on the cake. Dust with icing sugar. Chill for 1 hour. Eat on the same day.

Serves 12

PREPARATION TIME: 1 HOUR 20 MINUTES,

PLUS 1 HOUR CHILLING TIME

COOKING TIME: 50 MINUTES

OVEN TEMPERATURE: 160°C (325°F), GAS MARK 3

White Mousse Surprise

100 g (4 oz) plain flour, sifted

75 g (3 oz) cocoa powder, sifted

150 g (6 oz) caster sugar

225 g (8 oz) butter

50 g (2 oz) self-raising flour, sifted

2 eggs, beaten

150 g (6 oz) white chocolate

568 ml (1 pint) double cream

3 tablespoons (45 ml) brandy

50 g (2 oz) plain chocolate

25 g (1 oz) chocolate-coated peanuts

1 Grease and line a 20 cm (8 inch) round springform tin.

2 To make the biscuit base: mix together the plain flour, 25 g (1 oz) of the cocoa and 50 g (2 oz) of the sugar. Rub in half the butter. Using your hands, bring the mixture together and press it into the base of the tin. Place in a preheated oven, 160°C (325°F), Gas Mark 3, for 30 minutes. Leave to cool in the tin.

3 To make the cake: grease and line a 20 cm (8 inch) round straight-sided cake tin. Beat the remaining butter until softened, then beat in the remaining sugar, the self-raising flour, the remaining cocoa and the eggs, until smooth. Pour into the tin and cook at 160°C (325°F), Gas Mark 3, for 30 minutes. Turn out and cool on a wire rack.

4 To make the mousse: melt the white chocolate in a bowl set over a pan of simmering water. Set aside. Whip half the cream until soft peaks form. Carefully fold in the melted white chocolate. Spoon the mousse mixture on top of the biscuit base in the tin. Level the surface and chill for 1 hour or until set.

5 Place the chocolate cake on top of the mousse in the springform tin. Drizzle over the brandy and chill for 30 minutes.

6 To make the chocolate shapes: melt the plain chocolate in a bowl set over a pan of simmering water. Spread it over a marble slab or a cold metal baking sheet and chill for 10 minutes.

7 Remove the dessert from the tin, whip the remaining cream and spread it over the top.

8 Using a ruler and a small, sharp knife, cut out 8 diamond shapes of equal size from the set chocolate. Put the chocolate shapes on top of the cream and scatter over the chocolate-coated peanuts.

Serves 12

PREPARATION TIME: 1 HOUR, PLUS 1½ HOURS CHILLING TIME

COOKING TIME: 1 HOUR

OVEN TEMPERATURE: 160°C (325°F), GAS MARK 3

DEVIL'S FOOD CAKE

150 g (6 oz) plain chocolate

150 g (6 oz) butter

150 g (6 oz) soft light brown sugar

225 g (8 oz) self-raising flour

1 teaspoon salt

1 teaspoon bicarbonate of soda

150 ml (¼ pint) milk

2 teaspoons (10 ml) vanilla essence

2 eggs, plus 2 egg whites

450 g (1 lb) granulated sugar

1 Grease and line 2 x 18 cm (7 inch) round sandwich tins.

2 Melt 100 g (4 oz) of the chocolate in a bowl set over a pan of simmering water. Leave to cool slightly.

3 Beat together the butter and brown sugar until fluffy. Sieve together the flour, salt and bicarbonate of soda and beat into the butter and sugar mixture with the milk and 1 teaspoon (5 ml) of the vanilla essence. Beat in 2 eggs, one at a time, then beat in the cooled melted chocolate.

4 Divide the mixture between the 2 tins and level the surface. Place in a preheated oven, 180°C (350°F), Gas Mark 4, for 40 minutes or until a skewer inserted into the centre comes out clean. Turn out and cool on a wire rack.

5 Put the granulated sugar into a pan with 150 ml (¼ pint) water. Cook over a low heat until the sugar has dissolved, then boil for 3-4 minutes, until a teaspoon of syrup dropped into a cup of cold water forms a ball.

6 Whisk the 2 egg whites until stiff. Add the remaining vanilla essence to the sugar syrup. Pour the syrup, in a steady stream, into the egg whites, whisking continuously until the mixture is thick and stands in peaks. Use a third of this frosting to sandwich the cakes together. Use the rest to coat the top and sides.

7 Melt the remaining chocolate and put it into a small piping bag fitted with a no. 1 plain nozzle. Pipe chocolate 'webs' on to a piece of greaseproof paper and leave to set in the refrigerator. Use to decorate the cake just before serving.

Serves 10

PREPARATION TIME: 50 MINUTES

COOKING TIME: 40 MINUTES

OVEN TEMPERATURE: 180°C (350°F),

GAS MARK 4

PRALINE TRUFFLE

100 g (4 oz) caster sugar

100 g (4 oz) whole blanched almonds

775 g (1 lb 12 oz) plain chocolate

340 ml (12 fl oz) double cream

150 g (6 oz) unsalted butter

1 tablespoon (15 ml) rum

icing sugar, to dust

1 Grease and line the base of a 1.4 litre (2½ pint) loaf tin.

2 To make the praline: put the sugar and almonds into a heavy-bottomed pan. Cook over a low heat, stirring until the sugar has melted, and then cook for 1 minute, until it starts to turn golden. When golden, pour on to an oiled baking sheet. Leave until solid.

3 Meanwhile, melt 675 g (1½ lb) of the chocolate in a bowl set over a pan of simmering water. Remove from the heat and leave to cool.

4 Put the praline into a polythene bag and crush into small pieces.

5 Whip the cream until soft peaks form. Beat the butter until light and fluffy. Beat in the melted chocolate and the rum. Fold in the cream and the crushed praline. Spoon into the tin and leave to set in the refrigerator for 3-4 hours, or overnight.

6 Melt the remaining chocolate and spread it over a marble slab or a cold baking sheet. Leave to set. Draw a sharp knife at an angle across the chocolate to form curls. Run a warm knife around the tin to remove the cake. Pile the chocolate curls on top. Dust with icing sugar.

Serves 12

PREPARATION TIME: 45 MINUTES, PLUS 3-4 HOURS SETTING TIME

DARK BATTENBURG

225 g (8 oz) soft margarine

225 g (8 oz) caster sugar

4 eggs, beaten

150 g (6 oz) self-raising flour, sifted

½ teaspoon (2.5 ml) vanilla essence

65 g (2½ oz) cocoa powder, sifted

1 tablespoon (15 ml) milk

4 tablespoons apricot jam, melted

450 g (1 lb) white almond paste

1 Grease and line a 5 cm (2 inch) deep, 26 x 13 cm (10½ x 5½ inch) rectangular tin. Cut a 26 x 10 cm (10½ x 4 inch) rectangle of foil, fold in half lengthways, and use it to divide the tin down the middle.

2 Beat together the margarine and sugar until the mixture is light and fluffy. Add the eggs, a little at a time, beating well after each addition. Put half the mixture into a separate clean bowl.

3 Fold 100 g (4 oz) of the flour and the vanilla essence into one bowl and the remaining flour, 50 g (2 oz) of the cocoa and the milk into the other bowl.

4 Spoon the vanilla mixture into one half of the tin and the chocolate mixture into the other. Place in a preheated oven, 180°C (350°F), Gas Mark 4, for 30-35 minutes, or until well risen. Turn out and cool on a wire rack.

5 Trim the cakes to equal sizes and cut in half lengthways. Brush the sides with jam.

6 Fix alternate colours of cake together to form the main cake and press together gently. Brush the cake with the remaining jam.

7 Knead the remaining cocoa into the almond paste. Roll out on a surface lightly dusted with icing sugar to a 30 x 26 cm (12 x 10½ inch) rectangle. Put the cake in the centre of the almond paste, wrap the paste over the cake, and pinch the edges together to seal. Trim the ends. Put the cake on a serving plate with the seam side down. Using cake decorating crimpers or a fork, mark a pattern along the top of the cake.

Serves 12

PREPARATION TIME: 40 MINUTES

COOKING TIME: 30-35 MINUTES

OVEN TEMPERATURE: 180°C (350°F), GAS MARK 4

VARIATION

For a traditional yellow and pink Battenburg, use 225 g (8 oz) of flour and omit the cocoa and milk. Divide the mixture equally between 2 bowls. Flavour half the mixture with vanilla, and colour the other half with a few drops of pink food colouring. If you like, use melted, sieved raspberry jam instead of apricot. Cover with yellow or pink almond paste.

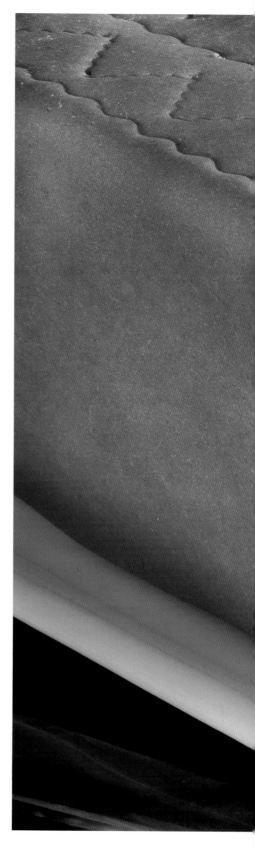

Pistachio Delight

215 g (7½ oz) plain flour

40 g (1½ oz) cocoa powder

1 teaspoon bicarbonate of soda

1 teaspoon salt

50 g (2 oz) bitter chocolate

325 g (12 oz) butter

225 g (8 oz) caster sugar

2 eggs, plus 2 egg whites

1 teaspoon (5 ml) vanilla essence

1 teaspoon (5 ml) vinegar

227 ml (8 fl oz) boiling water

325 g (12 oz) shelled pistachio nuts,
  toasted

150 g (6 oz) white chocolate

426 ml (¾ pint) double cream

100 g (4 oz) flaked almonds, toasted

1 Grease and line a 20 cm (8 inch) round deep cake tin.

2 Sift together the flour, cocoa, bicarbonate of soda and salt. Melt the bitter chocolate in a bowl over a pan of hot water. Stir until smooth. Leave to cool.

3 In a clean bowl, beat together 100 g (4 oz) of the butter and all the caster sugar until light and fluffy. Beat in 2 eggs, one at a time, then beat in the vanilla essence, vinegar and the melted chocolate.

4 Gradually fold in the sifted dry ingredients. Stir in the boiling water and beat until smooth. Pour into the tin. Place in a preheated oven, 160°C (325°F), Gas Mark 3, for 1 hour or until a skewer inserted into the centre comes out clean. Turn out and cool on a wire rack. Chill.

5 Reserve 16 pistachio nuts and chop the remainder. Melt the white chocolate in a bowl over a pan of hot water, stir until smooth, then leave to cool.

6 Beat the remaining butter, then beat in the melted white chocolate. Whisk the 2 egg whites until stiff, then fold in the white chocolate mixture and the chopped pistachios.

7 Using a long, sharp knife, slice the cake horizontally into 4 layers. Sandwich the layers together with white chocolate buttercream. Press the cake lightly so that the buttercream comes evenly to the edge.

8 Whip the cream until soft peaks form. Put a third of the cream into a piping bag fitted with a star nozzle. Spread half of the remaining cream around the side of the cake. Holding the top and bottom of the cake, roll the side in the flaked almonds. Spread the other half of the cream over the top of the cake and pipe rosettes around the edge. Decorate with the reserved pistachios. Chill for 30 minutes before serving.

Serves 12

Preparation time: 1 hour, plus
30 minutes chilling time

Cooking time: 1 hour

Oven temperature: 160°C (325°F),
Gas Mark 3

Strawberry Surprise

1.1 kg (2½ lb) plain chocolate

568 ml (1 pint) double cream

225 g (8 oz) unsalted butter

8 eggs

200 g (7 oz) caster sugar

675 g (1½ lb) strawberries

100 g (4 oz) white chocolate

1 To make the ganache: break 450 g (1 lb) of the plain chocolate into pieces and put into a pan with 340 ml (12 fl oz) of the cream. Bring to the boil and whisk until melted and smooth. Chill until required.

2 Grease and line 3 x 20 cm (8 inch) round cake tins. Melt a little of the butter and use to brush the tin linings. Put the remaining butter and 225 g (8 oz) of the plain chocolate in a bowl set over a pan of simmering water and melt. Remove the pan from the heat and stir until smooth.

3 Separate the eggs. Put the yolks into a bowl with 150 g (6 oz) of the caster sugar. Whisk until pale and thick. In a separate bowl, whisk 4 of the egg whites until they are stiff but not dry.

4 Fold the chocolate mixture into

6 To make the mousse: whisk the remaining 4 egg whites until soft peaks form. Gradually add the remaining caster sugar and whisk until stiff. In a clean bowl, whip the remaining cream until soft peaks form. Set aside. Fold the strawberry purée, whisked egg whites and whipped cream into the melted plain and white chocolate until the mixture is smooth.

7 Put 1 cake into the base of a 20 cm (8 inch) round deep cake tin. Arrange half the remaining strawberries on top. Spread over half of the mousse. Repeat the process with the remaining cake, strawberries and mousse, finishing with a layer of cake. Tap the tin 2 or 3 times on a work surface to eliminate air pockets. Chill for 1 hour.

8 Carefully turn out the cake. Whisk the ganache until soft and smooth and spread it over the top and sides of the cake. Chill for 20 minutes. Put spoonfuls of the remaining ganache around the edge of the cake. Decorate with the reserved sliced strawberries and sprigs of mint, if liked.

Serves 12

PREPARATION TIME: 1¾ HOURS,
PLUS 1 HOUR 20 MINUTES
CHILLING TIME
COOKING TIME: 40-50 MINUTES
OVEN TEMPERATURE: 160°C (325°F),
GAS MARK 3

the egg yolk mixture with a third of the whisked egg whites. Fold in the remaining whisked whites until no traces of white can be seen. Divide between the tins and level the surface. Place in a preheated oven, 160°C (325°F), Gas Mark 3, for 40-50 minutes, until a skewer inserted into the centre comes out clean. Turn out and cool on a wire rack.

5 Reserve 8-10 of the strawberries and cut into slices for decoration. In a food processor or blender,. process 100 g (4 oz) of the strawberries until smooth, then set aside. Melt the remaining plain chocolate and white chocolate in a bowl over a pan of simmering water. Remove from the heat and stir until smooth. Leave to cool.

NUTTY PYRAMID

450 g (1 lb) plain chocolate,
  roughly chopped

340 ml (12 fl oz) double cream

115 ml (4 fl oz) Irish cream liqueur

8 eggs

225 g (8 oz) caster sugar

225 g (8 oz) self-raising flour, sifted

25 g (1 oz) cocoa powder

75 g (3 oz) flaked almonds

1 To make the ganache: put the chocolate into a pan with the cream and liqueur. Bring to the boil until the chocolate has melted. Remove from the heat and whisk until smooth. Cover and chill for 30 minutes or until thickened.

2 Grease and line 2 x 33 x 23 cm (13 x 9 inch) Swiss roll tins. Put the eggs and sugar into a large bowl set over a pan of boiling water. Whisk for 5 minutes, or until pale and doubled in bulk.

3 Gently fold the flour into the egg mixture. Put half the mixture into another bowl and fold in the cocoa. Pour the 2 mixtures into the 2 lined tins. Place in a preheated oven, 220°C (425°F), Gas Mark 7, for 8-10 minutes, until golden and just firm to the touch. Turn out and cool on a wire rack and then remove the paper.

4 Cut each cake in half lengthways. Whisk the ganache until it is soft. Use two-thirds of the ganache to sandwich the 4 layers of cake together, alternating the plain and chocolate layers. Freeze for 1 hour.

5 Using a long, sharp knife, cut the cake in half diagonally to form 2 triangles. Use a little of the ganache to sandwich the 2 halves together, cut sides facing out, to form a large triangle. Trim the ends. Spread the remaining ganache over the outside and coat with flaked almonds.

Serves 10

PREPARATION TIME: **50** MINUTES, PLUS **15** MINUTES CHILLING TIME AND **1** HOUR FREEZING TIME

COOKING TIME: **8-10** MINUTES

OVEN TEMPERATURE: 220°C (425°F), GAS MARK 7

ESPRESSO FUDGE

150 g (6 oz) bitter chocolate,

450 g (1 lb) soft light brown sugar

575 g (1 lb 5 oz) unsalted butter

4 eggs, plus 5 egg whites

1 teaspoon (5 ml) vanilla essence

290 g (10½ oz) self-raising flour

2 teaspoons bicarbonate of soda

½ teaspoon salt

225 ml (8 fl oz) soured cream

115 ml (4 fl oz) hot water

225 ml (8 fl oz) double cream

250 g (9 oz) caster sugar

450 g (1 lb) plain chocolate,
  roughly chopped

1½ tablespoons instant espresso
  coffee powder

1 Grease and flour 2 x 23 cm (9 inch) round sandwich tins.

2 Melt 100 g (4 oz) of the bitter chocolate in a bowl set over a pan of simmering water. Remove from the heat and stir until smooth.

3 Beat together the brown sugar and 75 g (3 oz) of the butter for 2 minutes. Add 4 eggs, one at a time, beating well after each addition. Beat in the melted chocolate and vanilla essence.

4 Sift together the flour, bicarbonate of soda and salt and gradually beat into the chocolate mixture with the soured cream, beating all the time. Add the hot water and beat well. Pour into the tins. Place in a preheated oven, 180°C (350°F), Gas Mark 4, for 50-60 minutes, until a skewer inserted into the centre comes out clean. Cool in the tin.

5 To make the ganache: put the double cream, 25 g (1 oz) of the butter, 25 g (1 oz) of the caster sugar, 225 g (8 oz) of the plain chocolate and 1 tablespoon of the espresso coffee powder in a pan over a low heat and bring to the boil until the chocolate has melted. Whisk until smooth. Chill for 30 minutes or until thickened.

ESPRESSO FUDGE

6 Melt the remaining bitter and plain chocolate with the remaining coffee powder in a bowl set over a pan of boiling water. Stir until smooth. Leave to cool.

7 Beat the remaining butter until soft, then beat in the melted chocolate mixture.

8 In a bowl set over a pan of boiling water, whisk the 5 egg whites and the remaining caster sugar for 3 minutes. Remove from the heat and whisk until stiff. Fold into the chocolate butter mixture. Chill.

9 Slice each cake in half horizontally, then sandwich back together using a third of the espresso buttercream. Sandwich both the cakes together using half of the ganache. Put the remaining ganache into a piping bag fitted with a star nozzle.

10 Using a palette knife, thinly spread a third of the buttercream over the top and sides of the cake. Put the remaining buttercream into a piping bag fitted with a star nozzle. Pipe a ring of buttercream stars around the edge of the cake, then a ring of chocolate stars, alternating the rings until the top is covered. Chill for 30 minutes before serving.

Serves 12

PREPARATION TIME: 40 MINUTES, PLUS 30 MINUTES CHILLING TIME

COOKING TIME: 50-60 MINUTES

OVEN TEMPERATURE: 180°C (350°F), GAS MARK 4

COCONUT EXTRAVAGANZA

225 g (8 oz) butter, softened
225 g (8 oz) caster sugar
150 g (6 oz) self-raising flour, sifted
50 g (2 oz) cocoa powder, sifted
2 tablespoons (30 ml) milk
50 g (2 oz) desiccated coconut
325 g (12 oz) plain chocolate, roughly chopped
426 ml (¾ pint) double cream
25 g (1 oz) drinking chocolate powder
10 plain and milk chocolate-coated coconut bars
100 g (4 oz) strawberries, halved
icing sugar, to dust
10 fresh mint sprigs
100 cm x 1 cm (40 inches x ½ inch) green ribbon

1 Grease and line a 20 cm (8 inch) round, deep, loose-bottomed cake tin.

2 Beat together the butter, caster sugar, flour, cocoa, milk and 25 g (1 oz) of the desiccated coconut until smooth and fluffy. Spoon into the prepared tin and place in a pre-heated oven, 160°C (325°F), Gas Mark 3, for 55-60 minutes, or until a skewer inserted into the centre comes out clean. Turn out and cool on a wire rack.

3 To make the chocolate cream: melt 75 g (3 oz) of the chocolate in a bowl set over a pan of simmering water. Leave to cool for 2 minutes. Whip together the double cream and chocolate powder until soft peaks form. Using a metal spoon, carefully fold the cooled melted chocolate into the whipped cream and put half into a clean bowl. Toast the remaining desiccated coconut under a low grill and leave to cool. When cold, fold the coconut into half the reserved whipped chocolate cream.

4 To decorate the cake: slice the cake in half horizontally and sandwich together with the coconut cream. Place on a serving plate and cover the top and sides of the cake with the chocolate cream; smooth over with a palette knife.

5 Melt the remaining chocolate in a bowl set over a pan of simmering

water. Spread the melted chocolate on a sheet of nonstick baking paper to form a 25 x 23 cm (10 x 9 inch) rectangle. Leave in a cool place until just set. Using a clean ruler and a sharp knife, cut the chocolate into 15 rectangles, each 7 x 5 cm (3 x 2 inches). Leave until hard but do not chill.

6 Carefully lift the chocolate rectangles off the paper, handling them as little as possible. Press them into the chocolate cream around the side of the cake. Arrange the chocolate-coated coconut bars on top and then decorate with the strawberry halves. Dust the cake with icing sugar and arrange the mint sprigs on top. Cut the ends of the ribbon into 'V' shapes and tie around the cake just before serving.

Serves 10-12

PREPARATION TIME: **50** MINUTES, PLUS COOLING TIME

COOKING TIME: **55-60** MINUTES

OVEN TEMPERATURE: **160˚C (325˚F)**, GAS MARK **3**

DARK RUFFLE GÂTEAU

4 eggs, plus 3 egg yolks

100 g (4 oz) caster sugar

75 g (3 oz) plain flour

25 g (1 oz) cocoa powder

25 g (1 oz) ground almonds

100 g (4 oz) granulated sugar

75 g (3 oz) white chocolate

225 g (8 oz) butter, cubed

2 tablespoons (30 ml) chicory and
  coffee essence

50 g (2 oz) Amaretti biscuits, crushed

100 g (4 oz) plain chocolate

1 Grease and line an 18 cm (7 inch) square cake tin.

2 Put the 4 eggs and the caster sugar in a large bowl set over a pan of simmering water. Whisk for 10 minutes, until the mixture is thick and mousse-like. Remove from the heat and whisk until cool.

3 Sift the flour, cocoa and almonds on to the whisked mixture. Fold in gently with a metal spoon.

4 Spoon into the prepared tin and place in a preheated oven, 190°C (375°F), Gas Mark 5, for 30 minutes or until risen and slightly shrunken away from the sides of the tin. Turn out and cool on a wire rack.

5 To make the buttercream: dissolve the granulated sugar with 4 tablespoons (60 ml) water in a pan over a low heat, stirring occasionally. Bring to the boil and simmer for 5 minutes, until the temperature reaches 110°C (225°F) on a sugar

thermometer, or until a drop of syrup forms a thread when pulled between your thumb and forefinger (drop it on to a saucer first). Remove from the heat.

6 Melt the white chocolate in a bowl set over a pan of simmering water. Set aside.

7 Whisk the 3 egg yolks until pale and thick. Gradually whisk in the sugar syrup, whisking continuously until the mixture is cool. Beat in the butter until thick, then whisk in the melted white chocolate until the mixture is smooth. Stir in the coffee essence and chill for 30 minutes.

8 Slice the cake horizontally into 3 layers and sandwich together using two-thirds of the buttercream. Spread the remainder over the top and sides of the cake.

9 Press the Amaretti biscuit crumbs around the sides of the cake. Melt the plain chocolate in a bowl over a pan of simmering water and spread over a marble slab or a cold metal baking sheet. Leave to set for 5 minutes. Using a metal palette knife, pull across the top of the chocolate to form scrolls. Arrange the scrolls on the cake.

Serves 12

PREPARATION TIME: 1 HOUR, PLUS

30 MINUTES CHILLING TIME

COOKING TIME: 30 MINUTES

OVEN TEMPERATURE: 190°C (375°F),

GAS MARK 5

WHITE CHOCOLATE EASTER CAKE

150 g (6 oz) icing sugar
50 g (2 oz) cocoa powder
115 ml (4 fl oz) hot water
225 g (8 oz) ground hazelnuts
6 egg whites
100 g (4 oz) caster sugar
100 g (4 oz) plain chocolate
284 ml (½ pint) double cream
225 g (8 oz) white chocolate
100 g (4 oz) white almond paste

1 Grease and line 2 x 20 cm (8 inch) round deep-sided cake tins.

2 Sift the icing sugar and cocoa into a bowl and beat in the hot water until the mixture is smooth.

3 Dry-fry the hazelnuts in a small frying pan for 1-2 minutes, stirring frequently, until browned. Stir into the cocoa mixture.

4 Whisk the egg whites until stiff, then whisk in the caster sugar a little at a time. Fold a quarter of the whisked egg whites into the cocoa and hazelnut mixture, then fold this back into the remaining egg whites.

5 Divide the mixture between the prepared tins and level the surface. Place in a preheated oven, 180°C (350°F), Gas Mark 4, for 20 minutes, until risen and firm. Leave to cool in the tins, then turn out on to a wire rack.

6 Melt 75 g (3 oz) of the plain chocolate with 85 ml (3 fl oz) of the double cream in a small saucepan. Beat until smooth, then leave to cool. Use the cooled chocolate and cream mixture to sandwich the cakes together.

7 Melt the white chocolate in a bowl set over a pan of simmering water. Spread the chocolate evenly over a marble slab or a cold metal baking sheet and leave to set.

8 Whip the remaining cream until soft peaks form. Using a palette knife, spread the cream over the top and sides of the cake.

9 Draw a sharp knife at an angle across the set white chocolate to form curls. Use the chocolate curls to cover the cake.

10 On a work surface lightly dusted with icing sugar, knead the almond paste until soft. Roll out a quarter of the almond paste and stamp out leaf shapes; mark the veins with a knife. Shape little mushrooms from the remaining almond paste. Melt the remaining plain chocolate and dip the mushrooms into it. Leave to dry before using to decorate the cake, together with the almond paste leaves.

Serves 12

PREPARATION TIME: 1 HOUR

COOKING TIME: 20 MINUTES

OVEN TEMPERATURE: 180°C (350°F), GAS MARK 4

ALMOND GÂTEAU

90 g (3½ oz) ground almonds
240 g (8½ oz) caster sugar
8 eggs
65 g (2½ oz) self-raising flour, sifted
50 g (2 oz) granulated sugar
225 ml (8 fl oz) single cream
250 g (9 oz) unsalted butter
50 g (2 oz) icing sugar, plus extra
   to dust
2 tablespoons instant coffee granules
1 tablespoon (15 ml) boiling water
65 g (2½ oz) plain chocolate, melted
2 tablespoons cocoa powder
225 g (8 oz) white almond paste
mint sprigs, to decorate

1 Grease and line an 18 cm (7 inch) square cake tin; grease again.
2 Mix together the ground almonds and 100 g (4 oz) of the caster sugar. Add 4 eggs, one at a time, beating well after each addition. Using a metal spoon, fold in the flour.
3 Separate the 4 remaining eggs. Whisk the egg whites until stiff. Gradually whisk in 15 g (½ oz) of caster sugar. Using a metal spoon, fold the egg whites into the flour mixture. Spoon into the tin and place in a preheated oven, 190°C (375°F), Gas Mark 5, for 35 minutes or until firm to the touch. Leave to cool in the tin for 10 minutes, then turn out and cool on a wire rack.

Almond Gâteau

4 Meanwhile, to make the syrup: put the granulated sugar into a small saucepan with 4 tablespoons (60 ml) water and simmer for 2 minutes. Remove from the heat and leave to cool.

5 Whisk the remaining caster sugar with the egg yolks until pale. Put the cream into a saucepan and bring slowly to the boil. Whisk the hot cream into the egg mixture, return to a clean pan and cook over a low heat, stirring constantly, for about 2 minutes, until the mixture begins to thicken slightly. Pour through a sieve and leave the custard to cool completely.

6 Beat the butter until soft and smooth and then gradually beat into the cooled custard, together with the icing sugar. Divide between 2 bowls. Dissolve the coffee granules in the boiling water and beat into one half of the buttercream. Beat the melted plain chocolate into the other half. Chill for 30 minutes or until thickened.

7 Using a long, sharp knife, slice the cake horizontally into 3 layers. Brush each layer with a little of the syrup and sandwich the layers together with the chocolate buttercream. Using a palette knife, spread the coffee buttercream over the top

and sides of the cake. Chill for 30 minutes. Carefully dust the whole cake with 1 tablespoon of the cocoa.

8 Knead the remaining cocoa into the almond paste. Roll out thinly on a work surface lightly dusted with icing sugar. Cut the almond paste into long strips and arrange the strips in ruffles on top of the cake. Dust lightly with icing sugar and decorate with sprigs of mint.

Serves 12

PREPARATION TIME: 1 HOUR, PLUS
1 HOUR CHILLING TIME
COOKING TIME: 35 MINUTES
OVEN TEMPERATURE: 190°C (375°F),
GAS MARK 5

CHOCOLATE MAYO CAKE

250 g (9 oz) self-raising flour, sifted
1½ teaspoons baking powder
100 g (4 oz) cocoa powder, sifted
100 g (4 oz) hazelnuts, toasted and
  chopped
225 g (8 oz) soft dark brown sugar
200 g (7 oz) mayonnaise
225 ml (8 fl oz) boiling water
100 g (4 oz) soft margarine
125 g (5 oz) icing sugar, sifted
125 g (5 oz) hazelnut and
  chocolate spread
150 g (6 oz) milk chocolate
icing sugar, to dust

1 Grease and line a 20 cm (8 inch) round cake tin.

2 In a large bowl, beat together the flour, baking powder, half the cocoa, the hazelnuts, brown sugar, mayonnaise and boiling water. Pour the mixture into the prepared tin. Place in a preheated oven, 180°C (350°F), Gas Mark 4, for 55 minutes. Turn out and cool on a wire rack. Using a long, sharp knife, slice the cake in half horizontally.

3 To make the filling and topping: beat together the margarine, the remaining cocoa, icing sugar and hazelnut and chocolate spread. Sandwich the cakes together with half the mixture; spread the remainder over the sides of the cake.

4 Melt the milk chocolate in a bowl set over a pan of simmering water. Spread over the top of the cake. Chill for 15 minutes. Dust with icing sugar before serving.

Serves 12

PREPARATION TIME: 40 MINUTES, PLUS
15 MINUTES CHILLING TIME
COOKING TIME: 55 MINUTES
OVEN TEMPERATURE: 180°C (350°F),
GAS MARK 4

No-Cook Chocolate Cake

200 g (7 oz) plain chocolate

275 g (10 oz) chocolate cake crumbs

50 g (2 oz) shortbread, crushed

100 g (4 oz) hazelnuts, toasted and
chopped

50 g (2 oz) glacé cherries, chopped

3 tablespoons (45 ml) Tia Maria

75 g (3 oz) white chocolate

50 g (2 oz) puffed rice

25 g (1 oz) milk chocolate

25 g (1 oz) flaked almonds, toasted

1 Line a 900 g (2 lb) loaf tin with clingfilm, leaving it overlapping the top of the tin.

2 Melt 150 g (6 oz) of the plain chocolate in a bowl set over a pan of simmering water. Mix in the cake crumbs, shortbread, hazelnuts, cherries and Tia Maria.

3 Spoon two-thirds of the mixture into the clingfilm-lined tin. Make a dip in the centre of the mixture and spread some in a thick layer up the sides of the tin.

4 Melt the white chocolate in a bowl over a pan of hot water and mix with the puffed rice. Spoon into the tin and press in place. Spoon the remaining plain chocolate cake

mixture on top. Level the surface and chill for 2 hours.

5 Holding the clingfilm, pull the cake out of the tin, put it on a plate and peel the clingfilm away.

6 Melt the remaining plain chocolate and the milk chocolate in 2 bowls. Brush the top of the cake with 1 tablespoon of the milk chocolate. Scatter the almonds over the top and drizzle with the remaining melted chocolate.

Serves 12

PREPARATION TIME: 20 MINUTES, PLUS
2 HOURS CHILLING TIME

LUXURY LOG

4 eggs, plus 2 egg yolks

125 g (5 oz) caster sugar

75 g (3 oz) plain flour, sifted

90 g (3½ oz) cocoa powder, sifted

75 g (3 oz) granulated sugar

150 g (6 oz) butter, cubed

250 g (9 oz) plain chocolate

1.3 kg (2 lb 14 oz) white almond paste

icing sugar, to dust

13 fresh holly leaves

edible silver food paint

gold lustre powder

1 Grease and line a 33 x 23 cm (13 x 9 inch) Swiss roll tin.

2 Whisk together the 4 eggs and 100 g (4 oz) of the caster sugar in a bowl set over a pan of simmering water, until the mixture is pale and the whisk leaves a trail when lifted. Remove from the heat. Fold in the flour and 25 g (1 oz) of the cocoa. Pour into the tin. Place in a pre-heated oven, 190°C (375°F), Gas Mark 5, for 15 minutes, until well risen and slightly shrunk from the sides of the tin.

3 Turn the cake out on to a clean damp tea towel sprinkled with the remaining caster sugar. Put a piece of greaseproof paper on top of the cake and then roll it up loosely. Leave to cool on a wire rack.

4 To make the buttercream: dissolve the granulated sugar with 3 tablespoons (45 ml) water over a low heat, stirring occasionally.

Bring to the boil and boil without stirring for 5 minutes, until the mixture reaches 110°C (225°F) on a sugar thermometer or until a drop of syrup forms a thread when pulled between your thumb and forefinger (drop it on to a saucer first). Remove from the heat. Whisk the 2 egg yolks until pale and thick. Gradually whisk in the sugar syrup and continue whisking until cool. Gradually whisk in the butter until smooth. Melt 50 g (2 oz) of the plain chocolate and whisk it in to the sugar syrup mixture until thick. Chill until firm.

6 Unroll the Swiss roll and remove the paper. Spread half of the buttercream to within 1 cm ($^{1}/_{2}$ inch) of the edge of the cake and roll up. Cut a 2.5 cm (1 inch) slice and a large diagonal slice for the branch. Position on the cake board.

7 Roll out 100 g (4 oz) of the remaining cocoa/almond paste to a 15 x 5 cm (6 x 2 inch) rectangle. Repeat with 100 g (4 oz) of the white almond paste. Lay the brown rectangle on top of the white one and roll up tightly from the short end. Cut into 4 slices. Knead the remaining cocoa/almond paste into 450 g (1 lb) of white almond paste with enough cocoa powder to give a mottled, tree bark effect.

8 Spread the remaining buttercream over the log. Mould the spiralled almond paste 'wood rings' to fit the log ends and position on the cake. Thinly roll out the mottled almond paste and cut strips of 'bark' shapes. Lay the pieces on the cake, overlapping the edges. Press gently into the buttercream. Melt 50 g (2 oz) of the plain chocolate. Using a small plain nozzle, pipe a wood effect on the bark.

9 Wash and thoroughly dry the holly leaves. Melt 100 g (4 oz) of the plain chocolate in a bowl set over a pan of simmering water. Using a paint brush, coat the underside of each leaf with the chocolate. Put the painted leaves, chocolate side uppermost, on a wire rack and chill until set.

10 Make large and small ivy leaf templates from cardboard. Knead 25 g (1 oz) of the cocoa into 225 g (8 oz) of white almond paste. Thinly roll out 50 g (2 oz) of the dark almond paste and cut out 8-10 ivy leaves. Score the leaf veins. Repeat, using the remaining 50 g (2 oz) of white almond paste.

11 With the remaining 150 g (6 oz) of dark almond paste, mould 3 pine cones; press the rounded end of a piping nozzle over each. Melt the remaining 25 g (1 oz) of plain chocolate. Using a small plain nozzle, pipe veins on to the white almond paste ivy leaves.

12 Carefully peel the holly leaves away from the chocolate. Using a fine brush and silver food paint, paint silver veins on to the leaves. Before the paint dries, dust with a little icing sugar. Arrange the holly and ivy leaves on the log and the pine cones on the cake board. Dust the board with the remaining cocoa. Sprinkle a little gold lustre powder over the cake and leaves.

Serves 6-8

PREPARATION TIME: **30 MINUTES**, PLUS DECORATING TIME

COOKING TIME: **15 MINUTES**

OVEN TEMPERATURE: **190˚C (375˚F)**, GAS MARK **5**

5 Knead 15 g ($^{1}/_{2}$ oz) of the cocoa into 450 g (1 lb) of the almond paste. Roll out 275 g (10 oz) on a surface dusted with icing sugar and use to cover a dampened 30 cm (12 inch) round cake board. Trim the edges and knead the trimmings back into the cocoa/almond paste.

Not Quite So Naughty...

PERFECT PARKIN

50 g (2 oz) butter

50 g (2 oz) white vegetable fat

100 g (4 oz) soft light brown sugar

150 g (6 oz) golden syrup

50 g (2 oz) black treacle

3 eggs, beaten

142 ml (¼ pint) milk

100 g (4 oz) medium oatmeal

100 g (4 oz) self-raising flour

225 g (8 oz) plain flour, sifted

2 teaspoons ground ginger

½ teaspoon salt

1 teaspoon bicarbonate of soda

1 tablespoon golden syrup, warmed

1 Grease and line a 20 cm (8 inch) square cake tin.

2 Put the butter, vegetable fat, sugar, syrup and treacle in a large saucepan and melt over a low heat, stirring continuously.

3 Remove from the heat, then stir the beaten eggs and half the milk into the melted mixture.

4 Put the oatmeal, self-raising and plain flours, ginger and salt into a large bowl and make a well in the centre. Add the melted mixture and stir until well mixed.

5 Mix the bicarbonate of soda with the remaining milk, and then stir into the parkin mixture. Beat together well.

6 Pour the mixture into the prepared tin. Place in a preheated oven, 190°C (375°F), Gas Mark 5, for about 35 minutes, until risen and firm to the touch.

7 Brush the surface with warmed golden syrup. Leave to cool in the tin, and then cut into 16 squares. Keep the parkin in an airtight tin for 2 days before eating.

Serves 16

PREPARATION TIME: **25** MINUTES

COOKING TIME: **35** MINUTES

OVEN TEMPERATURE: **190**°C (**375**°F),

GAS MARK **5**

Beetroot Cake

450 g (1 lb) self-raising flour

1 teaspoon ground nutmeg

1 teaspoon ground mixed spice

275 g (10 oz) soft light brown sugar

100 g (4 oz) walnuts, chopped

2 ripe bananas, mashed

325 g (12 oz) fresh cooked beetroot,
    peeled and finely grated

4 eggs, beaten

284 ml (10 fl oz) corn oil

225 g (8 oz) half-fat cream cheese

75 g (3 oz) icing sugar

2 teaspoons (10 ml) lemon juice

mint sprigs, to decorate

caster sugar, to sprinkle

1   Grease and line a 20 cm (8 inch) round deep cake tin.

2   Sift the flour and spices into a large bowl. Stir in the brown sugar, walnuts, bananas and all but 25 g (1 oz) of the beetroot.

3   Make a well in the centre and add the eggs and corn oil. Beat well, then pour the mixture into the prepared tin.

4   Place the cake in a preheated oven, 180°C (350°F), Gas Mark 4, for 1½ hours. Cover with foil and cook for a further 30 minutes or until a skewer inserted into the centre comes out clean. Leave to cool in the tin for 10 minutes, then turn out on to a wire rack and leave to cool completely.

5   Trim the surface of the cake level. Beat together the cream cheese, icing sugar and lemon juice. Spread over the top of the cake. Using a ruler, make ridges in the topping. Decorate with the reserved beetroot and mint sprigs and sprinkle with caster sugar.

Serves 8

Preparation time: 15 minutes

Cooking time: 2 hours

Oven temperature: 180°C (350°F),
Gas Mark 4

Parsnip Seed Cake

325 g (12 oz) parsnips

225 g (8 oz) self-raising flour

1 teaspoon salt

1 teaspoon ground coriander

325 g (12 oz) soft light brown sugar

1 tablespoon caraway seeds

100 g (4 oz) desiccated coconut

225 ml (8 fl oz) sunflower oil

4 eggs, beaten

1 tablespoon clear honey, warmed

25 g (1 oz) preserving sugar

1   Grease and line a 20 cm (8 inch) round deep cake tin.

2   Peel the parsnips and coarsely grate them into a large bowl. Sift in the flour, salt and ground coriander. Stir in the brown sugar, caraway seeds and desicated coconut. Make a well in the centre and stir in the oil. Gradually stir in the beaten eggs, a little at a time.

3   Spoon the mixture into the prepared tin and level the surface with the back of a spoon. Place in a preheated oven, 180°C (350°F), Gas Mark 4, for 40-45 minutes, until well risen and golden. Leave to cool in the tin for 5 minutes, then turn out and cool on a wire rack.

4   Brush the honey over the top of the cake, and sprinkle with the preserving sugar.

Serves 8

Preparation time: 20 minutes

Cooking time: 40-45 minutes

Oven temperature: 180°C (350°F),
Gas Mark 4

SPICED BANANA BUNS

325 g (12 oz) strong plain flour

1 teaspoon mixed spice

pinch of salt

6 g (¼ oz) sachet fast-action dried yeast

40 g (1½ oz) butter, melted

1 egg, beaten

170 ml (6 fl oz) hand-hot milk

50 g (2 oz) sultanas

50 g (2 oz) banana chips

50 g (2 oz) soft light brown sugar

1 tablespoon apricot jam, melted

1 Grease and line the base of an 18 cm (7 inch) square cake tin.

2 Sift the flour, mixed spice and salt into a large bowl. Stir in the yeast and 1 tablespoon (15 ml) of the melted butter.

3 Make a well in the centre and stir in the egg and all but 1 tablespoon (15 ml) of the milk, to form a soft but not sticky dough.

4 Turn the dough on to a lightly floured surface and knead for 5 minutes, until the dough is smooth. Return to a clean bowl and cover with a damp tea towel, or put into an oiled polythene bag. Leave to prove in a warm place for 1 hour or until doubled in size.

5 Turn the dough on to a lightly floured surface and knead again until soft and smooth. Roll out to a 28 x 23 cm (11 x 9 inch) rectangle. Brush with the remaining butter.

6 Sprinkle the sultanas, banana chips and all but 1 tablespoon of the sugar over the dough, to within 1 cm (½ inch) of the edge. Roll up carefully from the long side, as you would to make a Swiss roll.

7 Using a sharp knife, cut into 9 equal pieces and place in the prepared tin. Cover and leave in a warm place until the dough doubles in size or reaches the rim of the tin.

8 Brush the risen buns with the remaining milk and sprinkle with the reserved sugar. Place in a preheated oven, 190°C (375°F), Gas Mark 5, for 20-25 minutes or until well risen and golden. Brush the buns with melted jam while still hot. Serve warm.

Makes 9

PREPARATION TIME: 25 MINUTES, PLUS 2 HOURS PROVING TIME

COOKING TIME: 20-25 MINUTES

OVEN TEMPERATURE: 190°C (375°F), GAS MARK 5

FRUITY MUESLI SQUARES

75 g (3 oz) soft dark brown sugar

100 g (4 oz) butter

4 tablespoons golden syrup

50 g (2 oz) desiccated coconut

50 g (2 oz) blanched hazelnuts, halved

75 g (3 oz) ready-to-eat dried apricots,
   roughly chopped

75 g (3 oz) pitted dates,
   roughly chopped

225 g (8 oz) porridge oats

50 g (2 oz) white chocolate

1 Lightly oil an 18 x 28 x 4 cm (7 x 11 x 1½ inch) shallow cake tin.

2 Melt the brown sugar, butter and golden syrup in a saucepan over a low heat.

3 Meanwhile, spread the coconut and hazelnuts on a grill pan, and toast until golden brown.

4 Using a wooden spoon, stir the coconut, hazelnuts, apricots, dates and porridge oats into the melted butter mixture. Continue to stir until the nuts, fruit and oats are evenly mixed and well coated in the buttery syrup.

5 Press the mixture into the prepared tin and level the top with a knife. Cover loosely with grease-proof paper and then chill in the refrigerator for 2 hours, until firm.

6 Break the chocolate into even-sized pieces and melt in a bowl over a pan of simmering water. Stir well and drizzle over the muesli mixture. Leave to set in the refrigerator for 15 minutes. Using a sharp knife, cut into 10 squares.

Makes 10

PREPARATION TIME: 20 MINUTES, PLUS 2¼ HOURS CHILLING TIME

CARROT CAKE

225 g (8 oz) butter, softened

225 g (8 oz) caster sugar

4 eggs, lightly beaten

225 g (8 oz) self-raising flour, sifted

grated rind and juice of 1 orange

225 g (8 oz) carrots, grated

100 g (4 oz) ground almonds

150 g (6 oz) low-fat soft cheese

75 g (3 oz) icing sugar

1 Grease and line a 20 cm (8 inch) round cake tin.

2 Beat together the butter and caster sugar until light and fluffy.

3 Beat the eggs into the butter and sugar mixture a little at a time, beating well after each addition.

4 Using a large metal spoon, fold in the flour, then stir in the grated orange rind and all but 1 tablespoon (15 ml) of the orange juice. Gently stir in the grated carrots and ground almonds.

5 Spoon the mixture into the prepared tin. Level the surface and place in a preheated oven, 180°C (350°F), Gas Mark 4, for 1½ hours, until well risen and golden or until a skewer inserted into the centre

comes out clean. Turn out and cool on a wire rack.

6 When the cake is completely cold, beat together the low-fat soft cheese, icing sugar and remaining orange juice. Spread this thickly over the top of the cake.

Serves 12

PREPARATION TIME: 25 MINUTES

COOKING TIME: 1½ HOURS

OVEN TEMPERATURE: 180°C (350°F), GAS MARK 4

No-Cook Fruit Slice

325 g (12 oz) shortcake biscuits

50 g (2 oz) ready-to-eat dried apricots,
  roughly chopped

25 g (1 oz) pistachio nuts,
  roughly chopped

25 g (1 oz) flaked almonds

2 eggs, beaten

1 teaspoon (5 ml) vanilla essence

25 g (1 oz) glacé cherries, chopped

25 g (1 oz) glacé ginger, chopped

200 g (7 oz) white chocolate

150 g (6 oz) unsalted butter

50 g (2 oz) plain chocolate

1 Line a 20 cm (8 inch) round shallow cake tin with clingfilm.

2 Break the shortcake biscuits into small, bite-sized pieces and put into a large bowl. Add the apricots, pistachios and almonds and stir to mix with the biscuits.

3 Beat together the eggs and vanilla essence and stir into the biscuit mixture with the chopped glacé cherries and ginger.

4 Melt 125 g (5 oz) of the white chocolate in a bowl set over a pan of simmering water. Melt the butter over a low heat and stir in the melted white chocolate. Stir into the biscuit mixture and mix well. Press the mixture into the lined cake tin. Chill for 4 hours, or until set and firm to the touch.

5 Melt the remaining white chocolate and the plain chocolate in separate bowls and then drizzle over the top of the chilled mixture. Chill for a further 30 minutes.

6 Ease out of the tin and mark into 12 sections.

Serves 12

Preparation time: 15 minutes, plus 4½ hours chilling time

VARIATION

If you can't eat uncooked eggs, substitute 115 ml (4 fl oz) orange juice.

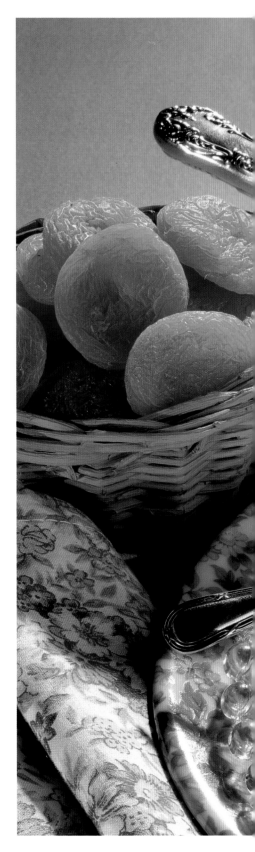

APPLE STREUSEL CAKE

1 Grease and line an 18 cm (7 inch) round springform cake tin.

2 Toss the apple slices in the lemon juice and set aside.

3 Beat together 150 g (6 oz) of the butter and 150 g (6 oz) of the sugar until light and fluffy.

4 Beat in the eggs, a little at a time, beating well after each addition. Fold in the self-raising flour, using a large metal spoon. Spoon the mixture into the prepared tin.

5 Rub the remaining butter into the plain flour and cinnamon, until the mixture resembles fine breadcrumbs. Stir in the remaining sugar and the chopped walnut pieces.

6 Pat the apple slices dry with kitchen paper and arrange on top of the cake mixture. Sprinkle the walnut mixture over the apples to cover completely.

7 Place on the middle shelf of a preheated oven, 190°C (375°F), Gas Mark 5, for 30 minutes. Cover with foil and cook for a further 45 minutes, or until a skewer inserted into the centre comes out clean. Leave to cool in the tin for 10 minutes, then turn out on to a wire rack and serve, warm from the oven or cold, with cream.

Serves 6

PREPARATION TIME: **25** MINUTES

COOKING TIME: 1¼ HOURS

OVEN TEMPERATURE: 190°C (375°F),

GAS MARK 5

1 cooking apple, peeled, cored and thinly sliced

1 tablespoon (15 ml) lemon juice

200 g (7 oz) butter

200 g (7 oz) caster sugar

3 eggs, beaten

150 g (6 oz) self-raising flour, sifted

75 g (3 oz) plain flour, sifted

1 teaspoon ground cinnamon

75 g (3 oz) walnut pieces, chopped

EASY FRUIT CAKE

397 g (14 oz) can condensed milk

150 g (6 oz) butter or margarine

275 g (10 oz) raisins

275 g (10 oz) sultanas

275 g (10 oz) currants

100 g (4 oz) pitted prunes,
   roughly chopped

275 g (10 oz) plain flour

2 teaspoons mixed spice

1 teaspoon ground cinnamon

1 teaspoon bicarbonate of soda

3 eggs, beaten

50 g (2 oz) walnut pieces

50 g (2 oz) stem ginger,
   roughly chopped

1 tablespoon apricot jam, warmed

450 g (1 lb) almond paste

cornflour, to dust

25 g (1 oz) blanched almonds

4 green glacé cherries

1 Grease and line the base of a 20 cm (8 inch) round, deep, loose-bottomed cake tin.

2 Put the condensed milk and butter or margarine into a large saucepan and heat gently until melted. Simmer for 2 minutes, stirring continuously. Remove from the heat and stir in the raisins, sultanas, currants and prunes. Leave to cool.

3 Sift the flour, spices and bicarbonate of soda into a large bowl. Make a well in the centre.

4 Add the eggs, walnuts, ginger and cooled fruit mixture. Beat well.

5 Spoon the mixture into the prepared tin. Using the back of a spoon, make a hollow in the top of the cake mixture. Place in a preheated oven, 150°C (300°F), Gas Mark 2, for 1½ hours. Cover with foil and cook for a further 15 minutes or until a skewer inserted into the centre comes out clean.

6 Cool in the tin. When cold, turn out the cake. If the top has risen, trim it level with a sharp knife. Turn the cake upside down and on to a plate. Brush with the apricot jam.

7 Roll out the almond paste on a surface lightly dusted with cornflour. Cover the top of the cake with the almond paste, and trim around the edge.

8 Knead the almond paste trimmings together and roll into 2 ropes, each 60 cm (24 inches) long. Twist together and wrap around the base of the cake.

9 Using a sharp knife, score a diamond pattern on top of the cake. Place under a hot grill for 3-4 minutes, until golden. Toast the almonds for 2-3 minutes, until golden.

10 Slice each glacé cherry into 4 and decorate the cake with cherry slices and toasted almonds.

Serves 12

PREPARATION TIME: 25 MINUTES

COOKING TIME: 1¾ HOURS

OVEN TEMPERATURE: 150°C (300°F),

GAS MARK 2

APPLE BRAN LOAF

100 g (4 oz) high-fibre wheat bran
   breakfast cereal

125 g (5 oz) caster sugar

150 g (6 oz) sultanas

284 ml (½ pint) milk

1 dessert apple

100 g (4 oz) wholemeal flour

½ teaspoon baking powder

1 Grease and line a 900 g (2 lb) loaf tin.

2 In a large bowl, mix together the wheat bran breakfast cereal, sugar, sultanas and milk. Leave to stand for about 30 minutes.

3 Peel, core and slice the apple and add to the soaked mixture with the flour and baking powder. Stir until evenly mixed.

4 Spoon the mixture into the prepared tin, smooth the surface level and place in a preheated oven, 180°C (350°F), Gas Mark 4, for 1¼ hours or until a skewer inserted into the centre comes out clean. Turn out and cool on a wire rack. Serve with butter, if liked.

Serves 12

PREPARATION TIME: 15 MINUTES, PLUS 30 MINUTES STANDING TIME

COOKING TIME: 1¼ HOURS

OVEN TEMPERATURE: 180°C (350°F), GAS MARK 4

APPLE MARMALADE CAKE

225 g (8 oz) soft margarine

150 g (6 oz) caster sugar

3 eggs, beaten

100 g (4 oz) thick-cut marmalade,
   warmed

225 g (8 oz) self-raising flour

450 g (1 lb) dessert apples, peeled,
   cored and sliced

icing sugar, to dust

1 Grease and line a 20 cm (8 inch) round springform cake tin.

2 Beat together the margarine and sugar. Beat in the eggs, then stir in the marmalade and flour.

3 Spread one-third of the mixture in the tin. Arrange half the apples on the mixture. Repeat the layering, finishing with cake mixture.

4 Cook in a hot oven, 190°C (375°F), Gas Mark 5, for 50-60 minutes, until the top springs back when pressed. Dust with icing sugar.

Serves 12

PREPARATION TIME: 20 MINUTES

COOKING TIME: 50-60 MINUTES

OVEN TEMPERATURE: 190°C (375°F), GAS MARK 5

APPLE FLAPJACKS

150 g (6 oz) butter

150 g (6 oz) soft light brown sugar

75 g (3 oz) golden syrup

325 g (12 oz) rolled oats

450 g (1 lb) cooking apples, peeled,
   cored and sliced

25 g (1 oz) caster sugar

¼ teaspoon ground cloves

1 Grease an 18 cm (7 inch) square shallow tin.

2 Melt the butter, brown sugar and golden syrup in a large, heavy-bottomed pan. Stir in the oats.

3 Turn two-thirds of the mixture into the tin and place in a preheated oven, 180°C (350°F), Gas Mark 4, for 20 minutes.

4 Cook the apples with the caster sugar and cloves until thick and pulpy. Spoon over the cooked flapjack. Spoon over the remaining oat mixture and bake for a further 30 minutes. Cut into 10 slices.

Makes 10

PREPARATION TIME: 25 MINUTES

COOKING TIME: 50 MINUTES

OVEN TEMPERATURE: 180°C (350°F), GAS MARK 4

APPLE SCONES

50 g (2 oz) butter

225 g (8 oz) self-raising flour

1 teaspoon baking powder

1 tablespoon caster sugar

25 g (1 oz) raisins

1 dessert apple, peeled, cored and
   finely diced

85-115 ml (3-4 fl oz) milk

1 tablespoon demerara sugar

1 teaspoon poppy seeds

1 Rub the butter into the flour and baking powder until the mixture resembles fine breadcrumbs.

2 Stir in the sugar, raisins and apple, then add the milk and mix to a soft but not sticky dough.

3 Roll out on a lightly floured surface to 2.5 cm (1 inch) thick. Using a 6 cm (2½ inch) cutter, cut out 10 scones. Place on a baking sheet and

brush with milk. Sprinkle with demerara sugar and poppy seeds.

4 Place in a preheated oven, 220°C (425°F), Gas Mark 7, for 10-12 minutes until risen and golden.

Makes 10

PREPARATION TIME: **10** MINUTES

COOKING TIME: **10-12** MINUTES

OVEN TEMPERATURE: **220°C (425°F)**,

GAS MARK **7**

Christmas

SPICE AS NICE

300 g (11 oz) currants

200 g (7 oz) sultanas

300 g (11 oz) large seedless raisins

100 g (4 oz) glacé cherries, halved

100 g (4 oz) candied mixed peel,
    roughly chopped

4 tablespoons (60 ml) cherry brandy or
    sloe gin

juice and coarsely grated rind of
    1 lemon

juice and coarsely grated rind of
    1 orange

225 g (8 oz) unsalted butter, softened

225 g (8 oz) soft light brown sugar

4 eggs, beaten

265 g (9½ oz) plain flour, sifted

1½ teaspoons ground cinnamon

½ teaspoon ground ginger

1 tablespoon mixed spice

50 g (2 oz) ginger in syrup,
    finely chopped

50 g (2 oz) blanched almonds, chopped

75 g (3 oz) macadamia nuts, halved

50 g (2 oz) luxury mincemeat

100 g (4 oz) white almond paste,
    coarsely grated

1 tablespoon (15 ml) liquid glucose

TO DECORATE

150 g (6 oz) white almond paste

75 g (3 oz) yellow almond paste

225 g (8 oz) caster sugar

50 g (2 oz) mixed unsalted nuts (e.g.
    brazils, cashews, pecans, walnuts)

50 g (2 oz) multi-coloured
    glacé cherries

100 g (4 oz) ready-to-eat dried apricots

4 cinnamon sticks

25 g (1 oz) piece of angelica

50 g (2 oz) assorted glacé fruit

2 tablespoons apricot jam

YOU WILL ALSO NEED

23 cm (9 inch) round gold cake board

cocktail sticks

assorted narrow ribbons

75 cm x 1 cm (30 inches x ½ inch)
    tartan ribbon

1 Put all the dried fruit, cherries and peel in a large saucepan with the cherry brandy or sloe gin and fruit juices and bring to the boil. Remove from the heat, cover and leave to soak overnight.

2 The next day, grease and line a 20 cm (8 inch) round cake tin with a double thickness of greaseproof paper. Wrap a double thickness of brown paper around the outside.

3 Beat together the butter and sugar until fluffy. Gradually add the eggs, beating well after each addition, and adding a little flour if the mixture starts to curdle.

4 Sift the flour with the spices. Beat the flour into the egg mixture until smooth. Gently fold in the soaked dried fruit, lemon and orange rinds, chopped ginger, nuts and mincemeat.

5 Put the grated almond paste in a bowl and, using a fork, stir in the liquid glucose. Bring the mixture together with your fingertips to form a soft, very sticky ball. Divide into 20 pieces and roll into small balls on a surface lightly dusted with icing sugar.

6 Spoon the cake mixture into the tin, randomly dropping almond paste balls into the mixture. Level

Spice as Nice

the surface and brush the top with a wet pastry brush. Cover with a sheet of foil with a 5 cm (2 inch) hole cut in the centre. Place in a preheated oven, 150°C (300°F), Gas Mark 2, for 3-3½ hours, until a skewer inserted into the centre of the cake comes out clean. (The skewer may come out slightly sticky if it goes through one of the almond paste balls.) Leave to cool.

7 To decorate the cake: knead the white and yellow almond pastes separately until soft. Divide the white paste into 12. On a surface lightly dusted with icing sugar, gently roll each piece of paste into a rope, 30 cm (12 inches) long. Divide the yellow paste into 6 and roll into 30 cm (12 inch) ropes. Plait 1 yellow and 2 white ropes together. Repeat with the remaining paste to make 6 plaits. Join 3 plaits together end to end and lay around the outside edge of the cake board. Place under a preheated hot grill for 3-4 minutes, or until the plait is golden. Leave to cool.

8 Carefully place the cake in the centre of the board. Join the remaining 3 plaits together and lay around the top edge of the cake in a 6-petalled flower shape. Place under a preheated hot grill for 3-4 minutes, or until the plait is golden, using foil to shield any areas that are browning too quickly.

Spoon the spicy cake mixture into the prepared tin, dropping in almond paste balls at random and making sure the almond paste is covered with cake mixture.

While the cake is cooling, make the caramel and coat the nuts, cherries and apricots, using cocktail sticks to dip them carefully into the caramel.

Cut the cinnamon sticks and angelica into 4-5 cm (1½-2 inch) lengths and tie together in neat bundles with narrow ribbon.

9 Put the caster sugar in a small pan with 6 tablespoons (90 ml) water and heat gently until the sugar dissolves, stirring if necessary. Bring to the boil and simmer without stirring for 10-15 minutes, until it forms a pale caramel. Meanwhile, firmly spear each nut and piece of fruit with a cocktail stick. Remove the caramel from the heat. Tilting the pan, dip the nuts and fruits in the caramel. If the caramel starts to thicken, return it to the heat briefly to melt slightly. Push the cocktail sticks into some potato halves to allow the caramel to dry. Leave to set for 1 hour.

10 Carefully cut each cinnamon stick in half and cut the angelica into matchstick-size pieces. Tie in bundles of 2 and 3 using ribbon.

11 Arrange the caramel-covered fruit and nuts, the cinnamon and angelica bundles and the assorted glacé fruit over the top of the cake. Fix the tartan ribbon around the cake board. Melt the apricot jam with 1 tablespoon (15 ml) of water. Sieve, then brush all over the top and sides of the cake.

Serves 20

Preparation time: 1 hour, plus overnight soaking and cooling time

Cooking time: 3-3½ hours

Oven temperature: 150°C (300°F), Gas Mark 2

STOLLEN

1 Put the flour, spice, salt, caster sugar and 125 g (5 oz) of the butter in a large bowl. Rub together until the mixture resembles fine bread-crumbs. Stir in the yeast, then make a well in the centre.

2 Beat the egg and milk together, then stir into the flour mixture. Mix to a soft dough, then knead on a floured surface for 5 minutes.

3 Knead in the fruit and candied peel. Put the dough into a bowl, cover with a clean damp cloth and leave in a warm place for 1 hour, or until doubled in size.

4 Turn out on to a lightly floured surface and roll out to a 30 x 25 cm (12 x 10 inch) rectangle. Knead the almond paste until it is soft and roll into a 30 cm (12 inch) sausage. Place in the centre of the dough.

5 Wrap the dough around the almond paste and seal with water. Place on a greased baking sheet, seam side down, and place in a pre-heated oven, 190°C (375°F), Gas Mark 5, for 35 minutes.

6 Melt the remaining butter and brush over the cake. Dust thickly with icing sugar. Keep for up to 2 weeks, wrapped in foil. Before slicing, dust again with icing sugar.

Serves 12

PREPARATION TIME: 25 MINUTES, PLUS
1 HOUR PROVING TIME
COOKING TIME: 35 MINUTES
OVEN TEMPERATURE: 190°C (375°F)
GAS MARK 5

400 g (14 oz) strong plain flour, sifted
½ teaspoon mixed spice
pinch of salt
50 g (2 oz) caster sugar
140 g (5½ oz) butter
2 x 6 g (¼ oz) sachets fast-action
   dried yeast
1 egg
170 ml (6 fl oz) hand-hot milk
50 g (2 oz) raisins
50 g (2 oz) glacé cherries, quartered
50 g (2 oz) candied mixed peel,
   roughly chopped
225 g (8 oz) white almond paste
50 g (2 oz) icing sugar

CHRISTMAS CAROUSEL

3 egg whites

675 g (1½ lb) icing sugar, sifted

20 cm (8 inch) round fruit cake,
*   covered with almond paste*

2 kg (4½ lb) ready-to-roll
*   fondant icing*

cream, red, yellow, green, brown and
*   black food colouring*

old gold edible food paint

YOU WILL ALSO NEED

30 cm (12 inch) round gold cake board

small paintbrush

stiff white cardboard and sticky tape

piping gun or bag set

1 First make the royal icing: put the egg whites in a clean bowl and stir with a fork to break them up. Gradually beat in the icing sugar and beat for 10 minutes, until the icing is white and forms soft peaks. Cover with damp greaseproof paper and put in a polythene bag. Leave in the refrigerator.

2 Put the cake on the cake board. Colour 900 g (2 lb) of the fondant cream, roll out and cover the cake. Leave to dry overnight.

3 Colour 675 g (1½ lb) of the fondant red. Roll out half the fondant thinly and cut out 8 rectangles, each 10 x 9 cm (4 x 3½ inches). Pinch each rectangle in the middle to give a draped curtain effect. Using a paintbrush and a little water, fix the curtains around the cake.

4 Cut a 29 cm (11½ inch) circle from the cardboard. Cut halfway through the circle and then make it into a cone 6 cm (2½ inches) high; fix with sticky tape. Roll out the remaining red fondant and use to cover the cone. Using a sharp knife, scallop the edge of the icing. Fix to the cake as a canopy, using a little royal icing. Leave to dry.

5 Trace 8 different shapes (e.g. snowman, crackers, plum pudding) on to greaseproof paper. Using a

small plain nozzle and royal icing, pipe the outlines and leave to dry for 10 minutes.

6 Thin the remaining royal icing with a little water, then divide equally between 5 bowls. Leave one white and colour the remainder red, yellow, green and brown.

7 Using a clean piping gun or bag and a large plain nozzle, carefully flood each outline with the appropriate coloured royal icing. Leave the figures to dry completely.

8 Roll out half the remaining fondant into 16 x 14 cm (5½ inch) lengths. Twist the lengths together in pairs to make 8 ropes. Using a little water, fix each rope from the top of the canopy to the bottom edge, between the curtains. Make 8 smaller ropes and 8 tasselled ropes and fix to each curtain.

9 Use all but 15 g (½ oz) of the remaining fondant to roll 16 thin strips, and fix around the scalloped

Position the curtains evenly around the cake, using a paintbrush and a little water.

Trace 8 shapes on to greaseproof paper and pipe the outlines in royal icing.

Carefully fill the outlines with the coloured royal icing and leave to dry completely.

Make the ropes by twisting together thin lengths of white fondant.

Paint the final details on to the decorative shapes with black food colouring.

edges. Paint the ropes and edging gold. Paint a gold border at the base of the cake. Paint the details on the royal icing shapes, then use the fondant trimmings to make extra decorations (e.g. leaves and berries). Fix to the cake with royal icing. Cut out a star from the remaining 15 g ($\frac{1}{2}$ oz) fondant, paint it gold and carefully fix it to the top of the cake, using a little royal icing.

CROWN OF HOLLY

4 egg whites

900 g (2 lb) icing sugar, sifted

20 cm (8 inch) round fruit cake,
    covered with almond paste

325 g (12 oz) ready-to-roll
    fondant icing

edible gold food paint

gold lustre powder

YOU WILL ALSO NEED

30 cm (12 inch) round gold cake board

holly leaf cutters (optional)

piping gun or bag set

small paintbrush

7 white candles

1 First make the royal icing: put the egg whites in a clean bowl and stir with a fork to break them up. Gradually beat in the icing sugar and beat for 10 minutes, until the icing is white and forms soft peaks. Cover with damp greaseproof paper and put in a polythene bag. Leave overnight in the refrigerator.

2 Lightly beat the royal icing, then use a palette knife to swirl a quarter of the icing over the cake board. Leave to dry for 2-3 hours.

3 Put the cake on the iced board. Reserve 3 tablespoons (45 ml) of the royal icing and swirl the remainder over the top and sides of the cake, to give a slightly peaked effect. Leave to dry overnight.

4 To make the holly leaves: roll out the fondant icing to a thickness of 3 mm ($\frac{1}{8}$ inch). Cut out 30 large and 20 small holly leaves using a shaped cutter. Alternatively, cut out 30 oval shapes, 5 cm (2 inches) long and 4 cm ($1\frac{1}{2}$ inches) wide, and cut out fluted edges using the wide end of a piping nozzle. Mark the veins. Cut out 20 smaller leaves using the same method.

5 To make the mistletoe leaves and berries: use the fondant trimmings to make 44 pea-sized balls. Roll 14 balls into cone shapes, then roll out into flat leaves. Mark a vein down the centre of each leaf and pinch the end to form a stem. For the berries, mark the remaining balls with the end of a paintbrush. Leave all the leaves and berries on crumpled foil to dry overnight.

6 Paint the edges of all the leaves with gold paint. Leave them to dry on a piece of greaseproof paper.

7 Using a paintbrush, carefully dust gold lustre powder over the berries and along the centre of the holly and mistletoe leaves.

8 Arrange 9 holly and 9 mistletoe leaves around the top of the cake; fix with the reserved royal icing. Mark the candle holes. Fix the holly, mistletoe and berries in the centre of the cake. Fix 12 holly leaves and berries in pairs around the side of the cake. Fix small holly leaves around the base of the cake. Put the candles in place.

If you do not have a holly leaf cutter, cut out the fondant and use the wide end of a piping nozzle to shape the holly leaves.

Use a small rolling pin or the handle of a small paintbrush to roll out 14 cone shapes to form the mistletoe leaves.

Plan where the leaves and berries should be positioned on the top, sides and base of the cake before fixing them with royal icing.

Winter Wonderland

6 egg whites

1.4 kg (3 lb) icing sugar, sifted

615 g (1 lb 6½ oz) plain flour

2½ tablespoons ground ginger

5 tablespoons blackstrap molasses

5 tablespoons golden syrup

75 g (3 oz) soft light brown sugar

125 g (5 oz) butter

1½ tablespoons bicarbonate of soda

2 eggs, beaten

100 g (4 oz) ready-to-roll
   fondant icing

red, yellow, green, black and brown
   food colouring

4 ice-cream cones, cut to various
   heights

20 edible silver balls

3 x 250 g (9 oz) boxes wafer-thin
   chocolate mints

20 red and green jelly sweets

1 chocolate Flake, quartered

icing sugar, to dust

50 g (2 oz) amber sugar crystals,
   crushed

You will also need

nonstick baking paper

scissors

cardboard

35 cm (14 inch) square silver cake
   board

piping gun or bag set

143 cm x 1 cm (57 inches x ½ inch)
   green ribbon

143 cm x 5 mm (57 inches x ¼ inch)
   red ribbon

dressmaking pin

1 Make the royal icing: beat the egg whites lightly, then gradually beat in the icing sugar; beat for 10 minutes, or until the icing is white and forms soft peaks. Cover with damp greaseproof paper and put in a polythene bag.

2 Sift the flour and ginger into a large bowl. Put the molasses, syrup, brown sugar and butter in a large saucepan. Melt over a low heat, stirring continuously. Stir in the bicarbonate of soda. Stir the mixture into the flour and ginger mixture and add the eggs. Mix to a soft dough.

3 Using a floured rolling pin, roll out half the dough on a large sheet of nonstick baking paper to a thickness of 5 mm (¼ inch). Cut out card templates for the gingerbread house (see illustration overleaf). Use the templates to cut out one of each main shape from the rolled-out dough. Reserve the trimmings. Lift the shapes, still on the baking paper, on to a baking sheet. Place in a preheated oven, 180°C (350°F), Gas Mark 4, for 10 minutes, or until golden. Leave to cool for 10 minutes and then transfer to a wire rack. Repeat using the remaining dough, and use the trimmings to make the chimney, door and shutters.

4 Spread 325 g (12 oz) of the royal icing over the cake board. Spread some royal icing along the edges of the chimney and chalet pieces. Press together the front, sides, back, roof and chimney. Leave to dry.

5 Spread the shutters with 50 g (2 oz) of the royal icing and

leave to dry. Colour 50 g (2 oz) of the royal icing red. Fill the piping gun or bag with the red icing and fit a small plain nozzle. Pipe 21 hearts on to some nonstick baking paper and then pipe red dots around the shutters. Decorate each of the shutters with 3 hearts. Reserve any remaining red icing. Colour 50 g (2 oz) of royal icing yellow and use to fill a clean piping bag or gun. Using a plain nozzle, pipe 21 bows and 4 stars on to baking paper.

WINTER WONDERLAND

To make the gingerbread house, you will need to make card templates: 2 rectangles 20 x 15 cm (8 x 6 inches) and 2 rectangles 18 x 10 cm (7 x 4 inches) for the roof and walls; 2 pentagons, base 15 cm (6 inches), 'walls' 10 cm (4 inches), 'roof' 14 cm (5½ inches). Make the chimney, door and shutters separately.

6 Colour 450 g (1 lb) of the royal icing dark green. Fill a piping bag or gun with 100 g (4 oz) of the green icing. Fit a small star nozzle and pipe 1 wreath on to the door and 1 on to some baking paper. Scratch scallop lines around the chalet with a pin. Pipe green swags along the pin lines and around the doorway. Pipe red berries on to the swags and wreaths. Using a little white icing,

fix 1 red heart on to the wreath on the paper. Decorate the swags with the remaining hearts. Fix 1 bow on to the door and the remainder on to the swags.

7 Colour the fondant icing appropriately and shape Santa's legs and sack, as shown below. Using a small star nozzle and the remaining green royal icing, pipe long stars to cover the 4 ice-cream cones to make the

trees. Leave to dry. Using a small plain nozzle and the remaining red icing, pipe bows on the large trees. Decorate all the trees with silver balls and top with yellow stars.

8 Using a small star nozzle and half the remaining white royal icing, pipe along the wall seams and the chimney top. Using a small plain nozzle, pipe dots around the windows and door. Fix the shutters, door and wreath in place with royal icing. Pipe lines along the roof. Fix the mint 'tiles' in place and pipe lines around the roof.

9 Pipe icing along the top of the roof and decorate with sweets. Using a large plain nozzle and the remaining royal icing, pipe around the eaves to create icicles. Position the trees and Flake 'logs', and dust with icing sugar. Fix on Santa's legs and sack with a little royal icing. Lay the sugar crystal path. Fix both ribbons around the board.

Stick the gingerbread house together with royal icing; leave to dry.

Make Santa's legs and sack from the fondant icing. Pipe elongated stars over the ice-cream cones to make trees.

Using white royal icing, pipe lines along the roof, then fix on the chocolate mint 'tiles'.

IT'S A GIFT

1.1 kg (2½ lb) ready-to-roll
   fondant icing
red and black food colouring
20 cm (8 inch) round fruit cake,
   covered with white almond paste
60 edible silver balls
edible gold food colouring

YOU WILL ALSO NEED

25 cm (10 inch) round silver cake board
3 cm (1¼ inch), 2.5 cm (1 inch),
   1 cm (½ inch) star cutters
75 cm x 5 cm (30 inches x 2 inch)
   red ribbon
60 cm x 1.5 cm (24 inches x ¾ inch)
   gold ribbon

1 Roll out 150 g (6 oz) of the fondant, dampen the cake board and cover with the fondant.

2 Colour 150 g (6 oz) of the fondant red. Roll out thinly and, using the 3 cm (1¼ inch) star cutter, stamp out 20 stars. Reserve the red fondant trimmings in a polythene bag. Roll out the remaining fondant into a circle large enough to cover the top and sides of the cake. Lay the red fondant stars randomly over the fondant circle. Using a rolling pin, gently roll the stars into the fondant. Put the cake on the board and dampen the almond paste. Carefully lift the fondant over the cake, smooth the sides and trim the base, reserving the trimmings in a polythene bag.

3 Press 3 silver balls into each red star. Using the 2.5 cm (1 inch) star cutter, stamp star shapes randomly into the icing. Paint the star shapes with gold food colouring (if it is in powder form, first mix the gold colour to a paste with a little water).

4 Roll out the red fondant trimmings and, using the 1 cm (½ inch) star cutter, stamp out 2 stars. Roll the remaining red trimmings into 2 ropes, each 80 cm (32 inches) long.

Position the red fondant stars on the white fondant circle, then gently roll them into place.

Twist the ropes together and fix around the base of the cake, using a little water. Roll out the remaining white fondant trimmings and cut out the label. Fix the 2 small red stars on the label. Paint your message in black paste food colouring and position the label on the cake. Tie a bow half way along the wide red ribbon and fix it to the cake with a little water. Fix the gold ribbon around the cake board.

Roll out 2 red fondant ropes, twist together and position around the cake.

GARLAND GLORY

1 egg white

225 g (8 oz) icing sugar, sifted

1.6 g (3½ lb) ready-to-roll fondant icing

20 cm (8 inch) round fruit cake,
  covered with almond paste

green, red, yellow and brown
  food colouring

YOU WILL ALSO NEED

28 cm (11 inch) round silver cake board

ruler

75 x 7 cm (30 x 3 inch) strip of
  brown paper

12 cm (5 inch) saucer

scissors

dressmaking pin

holly leaf cutters in various sizes

small flower cutter

cocktail stick

piping gun or bag set

175 cm x 1 cm (70 inches x ½ inch) red,
  green and gold ribbon

8 white candles

1 First make the royal icing: put the egg white into a bowl. Gradually beat in the icing sugar and beat for 10 minutes, until soft peaks form. Cover with a damp cloth.

2 Roll out 150 g (6 oz) of the fondant to a 28 cm (11 inch) circle. Dampen the cake board, cover with the fondant and trim around the board. Put the cake on the board and dampen the almond paste. Roll out 800 g (1¾ lb) of the fondant to a 40 cm (16 inch) circle and cover the cake with it. Smooth the sides and trim the base. Leave to dry.

3 Using a ruler, mark the brown paper at 15 cm (6 inch) intervals. Using the 12 cm (5 inch) saucer, join the marks to give a scalloped crown effect. Fix the paper around the cake. Mark the scalloped line with a pin. Remove the paper.

4 Roll 100 g (4 oz) of the fondant into a 95 cm (38 inch) rope. Drape the rope around the top of the cake,

following the pin marks. Fix to the cake with water. Leave to dry.

5 Colour 275 g (10 oz) of the fondant light green. Reserve 75 g (3 oz) and add more colouring to the remaining 200 g (7 oz) fondant to make dark green. Roll out the light green fondant thinly and cut into 2.5 cm (1 inch) and 1 cm (½ inch) strips. Cut 50 triangles from the strips. Make a cut in one side of each triangle and open out to form ivy leaves, as shown below right. Roll out the dark green fondant thinly. Cut out 125 holly leaves in various sizes; mark the veins with a knife. Curve some of the leaves over the handle of a wooden spoon. Colour 25 g (1 oz) of the fondant red and use to make 60 berries.

6 Roll out 75 g (3 oz) of white fondant thinly. Using a small flower cutter, cut out 43 Christmas roses. Use a cocktail stick to shape the petals. Colour 3 tablespoons of the

Using a paper template and a pin, mark a scalloped crown around the cake.

Following the pin marks, drape a rope of fondant around the cake.

royal icing yellow. Using a piping gun or bag fitted with a small plain nozzle, pipe dots into the centre of the roses. Colour 50 g (2 oz) of the fondant brown, form into 25 balls and shape the balls into fir cones. Mark with ridges and leave to dry.

7 Roll the remaining fondant into a ball, flatten and fix to the centre of the cake. Mark the positions for 3 candles. Use royal icing to fix some holly and ivy to cover the fondant ball, avoiding the candle positions. Fix on the berries, roses and fir cones. Mark the positions for the remaining candles where the rope meets the top of the cake. Cover the rope with the remaining leaves, berries and roses.

8 Using a star nozzle, pipe scrolls around the base of the cake. Fix 90 cm (35 inches) of ribbon around the board. Make 5 small bows from the remaining ribbon. Fix the bows and remaining candles to the cake.

Make ivy leaves from light green fondant and holly from dark green fondant.

Cut out white Christmas roses, shaping the petals with a cocktail stick.

Use royal icing to attach the leaves and flowers, covering the fondant rope.

WHITE CHRISTMAS

250 g (9 oz) butter

250 g (9 oz) caster sugar

1 teaspoon (5 ml) vanilla essence

5 eggs, beaten

150 g (6 oz) plain flour, sifted

150 g (6 oz) self-raising flour, sifted

juice of 1 orange and finely grated rind
    of 2 oranges

100 g (4 oz) ready-to-eat dried
    apricots, chopped

50 g (2 oz) blanched almonds, chopped

50 g (2 oz) toasted hazelnuts, chopped

100 g (4 oz) unsalted butter

225 g (8 oz) icing sugar, sifted

2 tablespoons (30 ml) orange liqueur

2 tablespoons apricot jam

900 g (2 lb) white almond paste

icing sugar, to dust

425 g (15 oz) ready-to-roll
    fondant icing

1.4 kg (3 lb) white chocolate-flavoured
    cake covering

brown, orange and red food colouring

¼ teaspoon gum tragacanth

20 cloves

150 g (6 oz) plain chocolate

75 g (3 oz) milk chocolate

21 kumquats

You will also need

25 cm (10 inch) round cake board

30 cm (12 inch) round cake board

4 straws

21 cocktail sticks

75 fresh holly leaves, washed

stiff florists' wire

red and green ribbon

1 Grease and line a 20 cm (8 inch) round deep cake tin. Beat together the butter, caster sugar and vanilla essence until fluffy. Gradually add the eggs, beating well after each addition. Sift the plain and self-raising flours together and add to the beaten mixture with the orange juice, folding in gently until the mixture is smooth. Add the rind from 1 orange, together with the apricots and nuts, and fold in gently. Spoon into the tin. Place in a preheated oven, 180°C (350°F), Gas Mark 4, for 1 hour. Cover with foil and cook for a further 50 minutes, until the cake is well risen and golden, or until a skewer inserted into the centre comes out clean. Leave to cool in the tin.

2 To make the buttercream: beat together the unsalted butter, icing sugar, remaining orange rind and the liqueur, until pale and fluffy. Trim the top of the cake to make it level and then slice the cake in half horizontally. Spread buttercream on the trimmed top surface of the cake, then turn it over and sandwich the two halves together. Stand the cake on the smaller cake board.

3 Melt the apricot jam with 2 teaspoons (10 ml) water, then rub through a sieve. Brush the jam over the top and sides of the cake. Knead the almond paste on a surface lightly dusted with icing sugar, then roll out to a 35 cm (14 inch) circle. Lift on to the cake and smooth down the sides, easing out the folds. Trim around the base of the cake and reserve the trimmings.

4 Mould a dome shape from 150 g (6 oz) of the fondant icing and fix to the centre of the cake with water. Melt the white chocolate-flavoured cake covering (do not be tempted to substitute white chocolate) in a bowl set over a pan of simmering water. Brush a little of the cake covering on to the centre of the 30 cm (12 inch) cake board and stand the smaller board on top. Stand the cake and boards on a wire rack and stand the rack over a clean tray. Pour the white cake covering over the fondant dome and allow it to run down the sides of the cake and over both boards.

5 Holding the wire rack and both cake boards, lift then firmly bang down on the tray several times until

Bang the cake and boards down over a tray to settle the cake covering.

WHITE CHRISTMAS

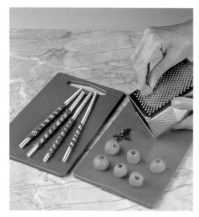

Create fondant curls by wrapping strips of fondant around straws. Roll balls of orange fondant against a grater to mark the fruit, and top each ball with a clove.

Holding the holly leaves by the stems, paint the glossy side of each leaf with melted chocolate. Leave to set on a wire rack, then add a second coat of chocolate.

Make bunches of berries by pushing small balls of fondant on to lengths of florists' wire and twisting the wire together.

the cake covering settles. Leave in the refrigerator until the cake covering is completely set. Scrape the excess cake covering off the tray and reserve it.

6   Colour 25 g (1 oz) of the fondant brown and knead in the gum tragacanth. Roll out thinly on a surface lightly dusted with icing sugar to a 12 x 2.5 cm (5 x 1 inch) rectangle. Cut into 4 narrow strips. Wrap each strip around a straw to form a corkscrew shape. Leave to dry overnight. Colour 100 g (4 oz) of the fondant orange and roll into 20 marble-sized balls. Roll each ball against the coarse side of a grater and push a clove into the top of each. Leave to dry overnight.

7   Melt the plain and milk chocolate in separate bowls over simmering water. Re-melt the reserved excess white chocolate cake covering. Push a cocktail stick into each kumquat. Dip 7 kumquats in the plain chocolate, 7 in milk chocolate and 7 in the cake covering. Push the kumquats into an orange and chill until set. Paint the glossy side of 40 holly leaves with plain chocolate, 20 with milk chocolate and 15 with some of the white cake covering. Place on a wire rack and chill for 15 minutes. Give the leaves a second coating and chill again.

8   Cut the florists' wire into 5 cm (2 inch) pieces. Colour 50 g (2 oz) of

the fondant icing red. Roll this and 50 g (2 oz) of white fondant into 60 pea-sized berries. Push the berries on to the ends of the wire and twist together into bunches. Dip the berries in melted white cake covering and in melted plain chocolate. Set aside.

9   Gently peel the holly leaves away from the chocolate. Remove the cocktail sticks from 17 of the kumquats and, using the remaining melted white cake covering, fix the kumquats, fondant oranges and chocolate leaves around the side of the cake. Push the remaining kumquats into the domed top of the cake to form a cascading shape. Fill in the gaps with chocolate leaves, fondant berries and fondant oranges. Gently pull the straws from the corkscrew shapes and fix to the cake. Fix the red and green ribbon around the bottom board, securing with a little chocolate.

Serves 20

PREPARATION TIME: 40 MINUTES, PLUS DECORATING TIME

COOKING TIME: 1 HOUR 50 MINUTES

OVEN TEMPERATURE: 180°C (350°F), GAS MARK 4

SANTA SPECIAL

Cut away a wedge of cake and brush the top of the cake with jam. Place the wedge on the other side of the cake to form a slope and brush again with jam.

3 egg whites

1.4 kg (3 lb) icing sugar, sifted

20 cm (8 inch) round fruit cake

3 tablespoons apricot jam, melted

900 g (2 lb) white almond paste

550 g (1¼ lb) ready-to-roll
  fondant icing

red, blue and black food colouring

YOU WILL ALSO NEED

25 cm (10 inch) round silver cake board

piping bag fitted with plain nozzle

1 First make the royal icing: put the egg whites in a clean bowl and gradually beat in the icing sugar; beat for 10 minutes, until the icing is white and forms soft peaks.

2 Cut a wedge away from half of the cake to within 2.5 cm (1 inch) of the base. Brush the top of the cake with 1 tablespoon of the jam. Flip

the wedge over and press on to the top of the cake to raise the 'slope'. Put the cake on the cake board and brush it with the remaining jam. Roll out the almond paste and cover the cake. Smooth around the sides and trim the base. Dampen the almond paste.

3 Colour 400 g (14 oz) of the fondant red. Roll out 250 g (9 oz) and use it to cover the raised part of the cake. Put the remaining red fondant in a polythene bag. Colour 125 g (5 oz) of the fondant pink. Roll out thinly, trim to form a 12 cm (5 inch) circle and lift it on to the cake.

4 Colour 15 g (½ oz) of the fondant blue and a pinch black. Make the features, using the blue, black and remaining white fondant, and the red and pink trimmings. Fix the features on to the cake with water.

Using a palette knife, swirl royal icing over the lower half of the face and the cake board to form the beard and moustache.

5 Spoon two-thirds of the royal icing on to the board and lower half of the face and swirl with a palette knife. Spoon a little royal icing into a piping bag and pipe the eyebrows. Roll out the reserved red fondant and cut a 20 cm (8 inch) triangle. Twist one point of the triangle downwards, and put it on the head. Swirl the remaining royal icing for a 'bobble' and hat trim. Using red food paste, paint on the cheeks.

SANTA'S SCENE

1 egg white

225 g (8 oz) icing sugar, sifted

1.8 kg (4 lb) ready-to-roll fondant icing

20 cm (8 inch) round fruit cake,
   covered with almond paste

1 teaspoon gum tragacanth

red, blue, pink, yellow, brown and
   black food colouring

old gold edible food paint

1 ice-cream cone

12 silver balls

YOU WILL ALSO NEED

30 cm (12 inch) silver cake board

small holly leaf cutter

piping gun or bag set

small star cutter

tartan ribbon

1 First make the royal icing: put the egg white in a clean bowl and gradually beat in the icing sugar; beat for 10 minutes, until soft peaks form. Cover with a damp cloth.

2 Roll out 150 g (6 oz) of the fondant to a 30 cm (12 inch) circle. Dampen the cake board and cover with the fondant. Put the cake on the board and dampen the almond paste. Roll out 800 g (1¾ lb) of the fondant to a 40 cm (16 inch) circle and cover the cake. Smooth and trim the fondant. Roll 75 g (3 oz) of fondant into 2 long, thin ropes. Twist together and fix around the base of the cake with a little water. Leave to dry overnight.

The fondant is mixed with gum tragacanth, so you need to work quickly before it hardens.

Make an effective Christmas tree by piping royal icing stars over an ice-cream cone.

3 Knead the gum tragacanth into the remaining fondant. (You will need to shape all the cake decorations within a few hours, before the fondant hardens.) Colour 250 g (9 oz) of the fondant red. Roll 20 g (³/₄ oz) each of white and red fondant into thin lengths, twist together and cut into 12 equal lengths for candy canes. Colour 40 g (1¹/₂ oz) of fondant dark blue and 40 g (1¹/₂ oz) pink, and take 40 g (1¹/₂ oz) of the red fondant; shape each portion into 5 presents. Colour 40 g (1¹/₂ oz) of the fondant green and stamp out 15 holly leaves. Use 15 g (¹/₂ oz) of red fondant to make the berries. Decorate the red presents with holly leaves and berries. Fill a piping gun or bag fitted with a plain nozzle with a third of the royal icing. Pipe the detail on the red and pink presents. Colour the remaining two-thirds of the royal icing green. Use a little of this to pipe the

detail on the blue presents. Roll out 15 g (¹/₂ oz) of white fondant and stamp out 8 stars. Paint them gold and leave to dry.

4 For the Christmas tree, use a small star nozzle and the remaining green royal icing to pipe long rosettes all over the ice-cream cone. Colour 50 g (2 oz) of the fondant yellow. Use 5 g (¹/₄ oz) of yellow fondant and 5 g (¹/₄ oz) of red fondant to make 12 tiny baubles of each colour. Decorate the tree with 8 candy canes, silver balls and baubles. Leave to dry.

5 Colour 20 g (³/₄ oz) of the fondant pink and shape Santa's head. Using 150 g (6 oz) of red fondant and 15 g (¹/₂ oz) of white fondant, shape Santa as shown below. Position Santa on the cake, starting with the legs, then attach the boots, body, arms, head and hat. Fix the belt and hands in place with water. Paint the hands, boots and belt

black. Paint the buckle gold. For the beard and fur, squeeze 15 g (¹/₂ oz) of white fondant through a piping gun or bag fitted with a fine mesh disk, and attach to the head and clothes.

6 Colour 90 g (3¹/₂ oz) of the fondant brown. Use 65 g (2¹/₂ oz) to shape Santa's sack. Put a ball of white fondant inside the sack. Roll out the remaining brown fondant and cut out 2 horses and 5 gingerbread men. Cut out a strip of white fondant and use trimmings of coloured fondant to make 4 xylophones. Use 40 g (1¹/₂ oz) of yellow fondant to shape 2 ducks. Knead the remaining yellow fondant with an equal amount of red to give an orange colour. Shape the ducks' beaks. Use 25 g (1 oz) of white fondant to shape 2 footballs. Paint on the design with black food colouring. Leave to dry.

7 Use the remaining green fondant to shape 2 trains. Colour 40 g (1¹/₂ oz) of fondant light brown to make 2 teddy bears. Colour 40 g (1¹/₂ oz) of fondant light blue and, using scraps of red and yellow, shape 2 jack-in-the-boxes as shown, left. Paint the details on the teddies and jack-in-the-boxes. Leave to dry.

8 Use royal icing to fix the tree and sack in place, then attach the presents and toys on the cake. Dust lightly with icing sugar. Fix the ribbon around the board.

Santa's body is made in separate parts, which are then put together on the cake.

Use a little water to assemble the toys, then paint them and leave to dry before arranging on the cake.

INDEX